MW00462051

Your Faith Has Made You Well

Preaching The Miracles

Cycle B

Charles L. Aaron, Jr.

CSS Publishing Company, Inc., Lima, Ohio

YOUR FAITH HAS MADE YOU WELL

Second Printing, 2005

Scripture quotations are from the *New Revised Standard Version of the Bible*, copyright 1989 by the Division of Christian Education of the National Council of the Churches of Christ in the USA. Used by permission.

Library of Congress Cataloging-in-Publication Data

Aaron, Charles L.
  Your faith has made you well : preaching the miracles, cycle B / Charles L. Aaron, Jr.
    p. cm.
  Includes bibliographical references (p   ).
  ISBN 0-7880-2367-5 (perfect bound : alk. paper)
  1. Jesus Christ—Miracles—Sermons. 2. Lectionary preaching. I. Title.
BT366.3.A17 2005
251'.6—dc22

                                                    2005009927

For more information about CSS Publishing Company resources, visit our website at www.csspub.com or e-mail us at custserv@csspub.com or call (800) 241-4056.

Cover design by Chris Patton
ISBN 0-7880-2367-5

This book is dedicated to my sisters
Terry Brewer Aaron Clarke
and
Stephanie Jan Aaron Gould,
to their husbands, Roy and David,
and to their children Devin, Sean, Alex, and Kaylee.

Acknowledgments

I would like to thank the congregations of the First United Methodist Church of Bowie, Texas and Cornerstone United Methodist Church of Garland, Texas. They participated in Bible studies and sermon series that helped me do the research for this book. Austin Presbyterian Theological Seminary provided quiet quarters for me to do the actual writing. Carol A. Miles of that faculty engaged in dialogue with me about the Gospel of Mark. Dr. Gene L. Davenport of Lambuth University, my first serious Bible teacher, read the manuscript. His many valuable suggestions improved this project considerably. Dr. Stan Purdum, of CSS Publishing Company, asked to me work on this book. I appreciate his confidence in me.

Table Of Contents

Preaching The Miracle Stories In Mark

Why Preach The Miracle Stories?

All four gospels in the New Testament exuberantly proclaim that Jesus performed miracles. Whatever we believe about these miracle stories, they present the preacher with a tangle of problems. As soon as we crack open our Bibles, we stare face-to-face with the issue of the historical reality behind the narratives. If we believe, as many do, that Jesus did not actually perform miracles — because miracles can't happen — then we assume the chore of explaining why the gospel writers recorded miracles. Are they simply pre-scientific attempts to understand psychiatric disorders and the psychosomatic dimensions of physical illness? Are the miracle stories metaphors or literary devices for a deeper spiritual truth? Should we discard them as Thomas Jefferson did from his version of the New Testament? If we believe that Jesus really did perform miracles, what do these stories teach us about our contemporary discipleship? Should we expect miraculous healings today? Should we counsel people with handicapping conditions and illnesses to expect that their physical conditions will be transformed in this life? If we believe that Jesus did perform miraculous healings, and that some people today are healed in ways modern Western medicine cannot explain, we still face the questions of what the miracles mean and why only some people experience such healings.

Once we get past questions about the historical reality of the miracle stories, we have to look at the needs of our contemporary listeners. If we preach that Jesus did heal and that God sometimes does heal, are we setting some people up for false hope, or (even worse) for a guilt trip that they were not healed because they did not have enough faith? If we preach about the miracle stories in the gospels, do we not run the risk of encouraging a kind of escapism, in which people argue about the historicity of the biblical narratives and miss the deeper theological significance of the stories? Too many people already understand faith as a valiant defense of the historical accuracy of the biblical narratives. Would preaching on the miracle stories in the gospels foster that attitude? On the other hand, if we "demythologize" the miracle stories, do we not encourage a view of first-century people as hopelessly naive dullards who readily believed in every miracle story that came along? Is there not a danger of exalting the modern scientific worldview if we see the miracle stories as only the "wrapper" for a deeper existential or spiritual truth? With such tricky obstacles to negotiate, we might decide to skip the miracle stories and preach the epistle lesson on the Sundays when the miracles come up!

Despite the many problems popping up around these stories however, they have great potential for proclamation. They have much to teach us about God's grace and about the ministry of the church. Such narratives enable us to wrestle with questions about the creation, providence, faith, and compassion. They help us reflect on our relationship to our bodies. These stories teach about the spiritual dimension to evil and its seeming intractability. They facilitate our reflection on suffering and the courage it can produce. How dare we ignore these stories with all their power waiting to be unleashed? With fair warning about the pitfalls, let us explore these strange but fascinating narratives and their possibilities for our preaching ministry.

An Approach To Reading The Miracle Stories

Reading the Bible has become a complicated task. So many methods of studying the text have arisen in the last few decades that even professional biblical scholars cannot keep track of all of them. A busy pastor can never hope to master all of the critical and post-critical approaches to the text. Preachers can learn from the results of scholars who use these methods with facility, but preachers need to study the text directly themselves. Even though we do not have a sophisticated understanding of all of the tools for reading a text, we can read the text with care and some intentional use of methods of analysis that the "pros" have developed. I want to advocate that pastors read texts with four basic concerns in mind: the background of the passage, the literary/rhetorical quality of the passage, the theological insights of the text, and the pastoral dimensions of the text. This approach to reading the Bible is not as complicated as it sounds, and it will yield a full, rich understanding of the passage for preaching. These four concerns in reading the text are not easy to separate. For example, the theological message of a text is often expressed in the development of the narrative itself. In that case, doing a thorough literary/rhetorical analysis of a passage leads to the passage's theological insights. Nevertheless, the preacher should ask explicit questions about each of these four concerns, so that none is neglected. Here, then, is a brief explanation of what I suggest about exploring these four concerns.

By researching the background to a miracle story, the preacher asks about what went before the text itself. What Old Testament narratives or ideas are reflected in the story? Does the story draw upon material from the intertestamental period or Greco-Roman writings? What do we know about understandings of medicine and health in that time and place? What sociological information about the background to the text is available to us? What can we know about the social situation of the early readers and writer(s) of the text? Although the evidence is strong that Jesus did indeed perform miraculous healings, we will not try to go behind the text in every case to determine exactly what happened historically in the life of Jesus and the early disciples. We will look instead at how Mark has used sources to interpret the healing ministry of Jesus.

A literary/rhetorical analysis of a passage looks at the text itself. This step in exegesis examines the artistry of the biblical writer. How are the characters developed? Which character is on a quest? How does the plot of the narrative unfold? What literary devices does the text employ? How does the individual pericope fit into larger units, including the gospel as a whole?

The theological interpretation of a passage continues the focus on the text itself. Even though the other interpretive tools help uncover the theology of a passage, in asking specific theological questions the preacher makes certain not to miss the explicit or implicit theological affirmations of the text. What does the text affirm or imply about God, the creation, the nature and ministry of Christ, the meaning of evil, salvation, or eschatology? What theological terms does the text use? What titles for Christ do the characters

9

use? Does Jesus fulfill the role of prophet, priest, or king in the narrative? What does the text teach about faith, the Christian life, or the mission of the church?

Reflecting on the pastoral dimensions of a text examines the interaction between the text and the contemporary situation. Pastoral exegesis of a text is highly intuitive and must be done with care. We want to reflect on how we can empathize with the characters in the text, but we don't want to read anything into the text. In pastoral exegesis, the preacher asks about the emotions implicit in the narrative. How might it feel to be a leper? Pastoral exegesis asks what insight the text might give about the human condition. How do we experience and cope with suffering? How do we relate to our bodies? What is our relationship to nature and to each other? Part of pastoral exegesis is to ask about power relationships in the text. Who wields power, and who is victimized by power? What insights does the text give for imbalances of power in contemporary society?

Although we will not examine every question mentioned under these four concerns of the interpreter, we will look at the miracle stories in Mark with these issues in mind. It is hoped that such an approach will yield a holistic understanding of each passage.

What Do We Mean By Healing?

I am not a physician or a scientist, so I cannot speak with authority about how modern western medicine understands health, illness, or disability. With that disclaimer in mind, I want to suggest that we can talk about healing in at least four ways.

The first way is the most obvious way, that God changes the physical condition of a person with an illness or handicapping condition. A blind person sees; a lame person walks; a person with cancer becomes free of the disease. This is the way our stories in Mark portray Jesus' miraculous healings. I do not want to spend a lot of time talking about whether miracles work outside the laws of nature or whether we just don't understand those laws yet. I believe that Jesus' ministry included acts of healing that should be interpreted as God's direct intervention as evidence of God's grace. These acts of healing were not consistent with the understanding

10

of nature held by the first-century observers of the acts, by the initial readers of Mark, or by contemporary people.

People today also report such healings. *Newsweek* magazine tells the story of Bernadette McKenzie, who, at the age of 12, was inexplicably cured of a tethered spinal cord. She was unable to stand upright and was in unceasing pain. The nuns at her Catholic high school were praying to Mother Frances de Sales Aviat for her recovery. Bernadette herself knelt by her bed one night for prayer. She asked for evidence that God would hear her prayer. Specifically, she asked that the next song on the radio would be "Forever Young." When that song came up next on the radio, Bernadette raced downstairs to tell her parents, oblivious to the fact that running down the stairs meant she had indeed been cured. Her physicians cannot explain her healing.[1] Enough such reports have been offered that preachers and the church should take them seriously. Part of the preacher's task is to help the church interpret such accounts.

Although these accounts of miraculous healings seem to be the most direct link between the stories of Jesus' healings and the contemporary situation, they are not the only way we can understand healing. One of the concerns of this book is to enable preachers to interpret these stories for people who do not have handicapping conditions. With that in mind, we can talk about the other ways to understand healing.

A second way to understand healing is to acknowledge the link between faith and wellness. Much research indicates that people who are observant in their religious practices are healthier than those who don't. Beside the benefits of a presumed healthier lifestyle (less alcohol, for example) the observance of religious practices itself seems to promote health. Prayer, scripture reading, a hopeful outlook, and other observances of religious practice tend to have a physiological effect, as seen in such indicators as lower blood pressure, more rapid recovery from surgery and even longer life expectancy.[2] The exact relationship between faith and wellness cannot be quantified, but the preacher can still speak responsibly about this understanding of healing.

11

A third and quite common way to talk about healing is to affirm that the ability to cope with strength, courage, and serenity in the face of disabilities and illnesses is also a gift of the grace of God. A popular slogan expresses this understanding: "Healing does not always mean a cure." Obviously, in the miracle stories of the gospels, Jesus does not offer this kind of healing. Jesus transforms the physical condition of the person who has come or been brought to him. Nevertheless, gaining courage and a sense of peace in the face of a physical condition that will not change is a true gift from God and is not easily attained. In all likelihood, the Apostle Paul refers to this kind of healing when he assures the Corinthian church that God's grace enables him to continue his ministry despite a "thorn" that will not go away. As Paul tells the Corinthians, "Three times I appealed to the Lord about this, that it would leave me, but he said to me, 'My grace is sufficient for you, for my power is made perfect in weakness' " (2 Corinthians 12:8-9). Even though we do not know for sure that Paul's "thorn" was a physical problem, the attitude is the same. Paul will rely on God's grace to cope with what will not change.

As we will discuss below, preachers must be careful not to induce guilt in people who cannot maintain a courageous attitude. To proclaim healing as courageous acceptance of injury or illness is not insistence on "suffering in silence" or dismissing people's frustrations with calls to "deal with it," or "get over it." Preachers must take care to lead people to the position of courage in the face of suffering. Acceptance of an illness or handicapping condition may take time, prayer, and effort. It may not be a static condition that, once achieved, never wavers. The church can be a supportive community as people open themselves to God's grace to bear up under a condition that will not change.

Finally, in connection with the healing stories in the gospels, we can talk about the church's ministry in health care, community support, missions, and advocacy of justice. The church performs a variety of ministries connected with health and disability. The church sponsors health clinics, sends medical missionaries, collects eyeglasses and hearing aids, raises money for a variety of causes, and holds blood drives, just to name a few activities. In

12

addition to its efforts to alleviate suffering, the church works for justice on behalf of people with health problems and handicapping conditions. The church should support efforts to make all facilities accessible and should work for dignity and full employment for people who can work, but who face barriers because of health conditions. The church should be in the forefront of efforts to change attitudes toward people with handicapping conditions. Part of that effort is to use care in choosing words to describe people with disabilities and the disabilities themselves. Even the use of the term "disabilities" carries some connotation of limitations. We want to be careful and sensitive in how we talk about handicapping conditions. We especially want to avoid words that demean others or that identify people by their handicapping situation. Some people with physical limitations are troubled by the miracle stories in the gospels because the interpretations of these stories have suggested that limitations imply the absence of God's favor or a lack of faith. I want to respect the unique circumstances of people with physical limitations and illnesses, while also affirming that the miracle stories in Mark communicate God's grace to all of us.

Understanding The Miracles Within The Gospel of Mark

The miracle stories in the Gospel of Mark are not just isolated, independent narratives. They fit into the whole message of the gospel. Although I will not attempt here a full treatment of the theology of the Gospel of Mark, some key verses indicate the substance of Mark's message and some tensions within that message. At least a basic understanding of that message is important for a responsible interpretation of the miracle stories.

Mark 1:14-15 is one such key verse. "Now after John was arrested, Jesus came to Galilee, proclaiming the good news of God, and saying, 'The time is fulfilled, and the kingdom of God has come near; repent, and believe in the good news.' " In two earlier verses, Jesus has been identified as the Son of God (Mark 1:1, 11). Verses 14-15 help us interpret Jesus' mission. Jesus embodies the coming near of the dominion of God. The dominion (or kingdom) of God refers to the completion and redemption of God's creation. God intended the creation to exist in harmony, peace (shalom),

13

justice, and wholeness. The powers of sin, death, and evil have corrupted God's good creation. Jesus' mission is to announce and make manifest that the dominion of God has not come in its fullness, but has come near. (No one biblical book, including Mark, gives a full explication of the dominion of God, but see Romans 8:18-21.) In the ministry of Jesus, the dominion of God has broken into the current creation, and Jesus' healings and exorcisms are part of that in-breaking. As such, Jesus' healings and miracles are eschatological. They indicate the wholeness and justice that will characterize the dominion of God in its fullness.

Jesus' ministry embodies the in-breaking of the dominion of God, but Jesus encounters resistance from both human and demonic forces. The allusion to the arrest of John the Baptist in Mark 1:14 foreshadows this resistance. The resistance to Jesus' ministry is woven throughout the Gospel of Mark. A summary of this resistance is found in Mark 8:31-38. In this passage, Jesus predicts his own death and calls his followers to take up their crosses. Obviously, this theme stands in tension with the life and health-giving miracles of Jesus. Part of Jesus' ministry is also to stand with integrity against the evil of the world. That integrity will lead to his death. In preaching the miracle stories, we must not treat health and physical wholeness as ends in themselves. Even though observing religious practices can make us healthier (lower blood pressure and all that), a genuine attempt to live out our faith may lead to taking up our crosses and laying down our lives! The fact that the evil of the world (human and demonic) is capable of killing Jesus is evidence that the dominion of God has not come in its fullness.

Part of the mission of the church is to bear witness that, in Jesus, the dominion of God has come near. That witness includes the affirmation that God's grace offers wholeness, now and in the completeness of the dominion of God. The church continues Jesus' ministry of proclaiming and embodying God's renewal of creation. The church's witness also includes the call to take up our cross and to be a servant (Mark 10:41-45). Mark would not want us to separate the miracle stories from the call to take up our cross. To preach only the miracle stories without the call to discipleship and service

14

would run the risk of reducing the church's witness to fulfilling our own indulgence and the meeting of our own needs. To neglect to preach the miracle stories while calling for believers to take up their crosses would run the risk of reducing the church's witness to a dreary call to sacrifice without the good news of God's remarkable grace.

---

1. Kenneth L. Woodward, "What Miracles Mean" *Newsweek* magazine, May 1, 2000, pp. 55-56.

2. Claudia Kalb "Faith and Healing," *Newsweek* magazine, November 1, 2003, pp. 44-56.

Miracle One

Jesus Meets The Official Spokesdemon

The Text

They went to Capernaum; and when the sabbath came, he entered the synagogue and taught. They were astounded at his teaching, for he taught them as one having authority, and not as the scribes. Just then there was in their synagogue a man with an unclean spirit, and he cried out, "What have you to do with us, Jesus of Nazareth? Have you come to destroy us? I know who you are, the Holy One of God." But Jesus rebuked him, saying, "Be silent, and come out of him!" And the unclean spirit, convulsing him and crying with a loud voice, came out of him. They were all amazed, and they kept on asking one another, "What is this? A new teaching — with authority! He commands even the unclean spirits, and they obey him." At once his fame began to spread throughout the surrounding region of Galilee.

Most pastors begin their ministry with a warm welcome. Best behavior and friendliness are the order of the day among the laity of the new church. Pastor, spouse, and children (if any) usually sit down to a potluck dinner in a freshly scrubbed and decorated fellowship hall. The leaders of the church may make a speech, gushing about how happy the church is to receive the new pastor. All in all, the day of a pastor's first sermon usually is filled with bright smiles, firm handshakes, and best wishes. At the beginning of Jesus' ministry, he is greeted by a man with an unclean spirit.

By having Jesus confront a man with an unclean spirit right up front, the Gospel of Mark dives into the action. With no birth stories or genealogies, Mark rushes to Jesus' adult ministry. With a brief account of the ministry of John the Baptist and a bare-bones description of Jesus' baptism and temptation, Mark puts us into the thick of the fight by verse 21. Mark's spare description and immediacy convey a sense of urgency throughout the gospel. This first miracle helps to set the tone for the gospel, and helps us understand Jesus' ministry.

Background

This narrative describes a man "with an unclean spirit." We infer from the description in Mark that this spirit is a non-corporal entity which is somehow "inside" the man, and controls, at least, his movements and speech. Mark does not tell us how the demon got inside the man, or what has happened to the man's personality during the indwelling of the unclean spirit. We don't know if the man could or did try to resist the spirit or for how long the spirit had been inside him.

If we search the Old Testament for stories that describe exactly the same kind of phenomena, we will not find them. The Old Testament does not contain stories of unclean spirits who invade a person's body. Nevertheless, the Old Testament does contain stories of people who have been influenced by otherworldly beings, including God. Some of these stories may give us insights into this story in Mark.

In 1 Kings 22, King Ahab of Israel and King Jehoshaphat of Judah want to go to war with Aram over the territory of Ramoth-Gilead. As part of the preparation for war, the kings consult Ahab's "advisors," the prophets. The official prophets tell the kings to go to war, because they will surely prevail. Finally, they consult the true prophet, Micaiah ben Imlah, even though Ahab doesn't like him. Micaiah taunts the kings with a false prediction of victory. When the kings press him, he tells them that, in a vision, he "saw all Israel scattered on the mountains, like sheep that have no shepherd" (1 Kings 22:17). Then Micaiah tells them that in another vision he saw the host of heaven sitting with the Lord. A "lying spirit" volunteered to influence the prophets to give a false prophecy of victory to Ahab. This passage does not indicate that the "lying spirit" was "inside" the prophets, but the spirit clearly influenced their speech. According to Micaiah's vision, not only did the Lord approve the plan, but was even the one who asked for volunteers to begin with! Clearly, even though the lying spirit could influence human action, it did not oppose the will of God. Causing the official prophets to lie was God's will.

1 Samuel 16:14 recounts the experience of King Saul. Because of Saul's disobedience and failure, the Lord has "rejected" him as king of Israel (16:1). The prophet-priest Samuel has hand picked David as Saul's successor. Verse 14 says that "the spirit of the Lord departed from Saul (see 1 Samuel 10:10), and an evil spirit from the Lord tormented him." The "evil spirit" from the Lord seems to have been a kind of depression, because the text says that Saul's counselors invited David to play the lyre for him, so that he will "feel better." If our inference is correct that Saul suffered from depression, then this text represents an early interpretation of a psychological illness being attributed to an outside "spirit." The passage does not indicate that the spirit blocked Saul's personality, as the unclean spirit seems to do in Mark 1. The evil spirit came from "the Lord," so it was not an entity that sought to oppose God's will.

A third story comes closest of all to a parallel with Mark 1. In 1 Chronicles 21:1, Satan "incited David to count the people of Israel." In Satan's few appearances in the Old Testament he is usually a member of the Lord's court in heaven, often serving as an accuser (see Zechariah 3:1-2). A sense of rivalry exists between the Lord and Satan in the first chapter of Job, but Satan is fully under the Lord's control. 1 Chronicles 21 does not tell us much about Satan, but it is clear that he can influence David's decisions. The text does not indicate how Satan was able to "incite" David, but he does not seem to have gotten inside David. God is displeased at the census (1 Chronicles 21:7).[1] Nevertheless, David takes responsibility (21:8).

These three examples indicate that the Old Testament contained the idea of an outside, spiritual entity influencing human behavior.

A gap still exists between these stories and the account in Mark about an unclean spirit inhabiting a person. Accounts of demon habitation begin to appear in Jewish literature during the intertestamental period. Perhaps these accounts were influenced by Zoroastrianism, which had a well-developed demonology. By the time the New Testament was written, belief in demon possession and exorcism were commonly accepted.

The preacher may wish to check some other Old Testament references to demons, even though these passages do not refer to demons inhabiting a person. A few texts refer to making sacrifices to demons: Deuteronomy 32:17; Leviticus 17:7; and Psalm 106:37. A handful of texts allude to "goat-demons": 2 Chronicles 11:15; Leviticus 17:7. Psalm 78:49 mentions "destroying angels." Some texts seem to personify pestilence: Psalm 91:5; Habakkuk 3:5; and Deuteronomy 32:24.

This brief historical look at the background to the unclean spirit in this passage indicates that the Bible consistently affirms that some kinds of spiritual entities exist and bear some responsibility for evil and suffering. These entities can influence human behavior and decisions. The understanding of demons and unclean spirits that lies behind this passage developed after the writing of the Old Testament. That the understanding of demons evolved within the Old Testament and the intertestamental literature makes precise definitions of demons and statements about the exact origin of demons impossible to formulate. Demons were spiritual beings that opposed God's will and could influence human behavior.

Literary Analysis

Now that Jesus has been baptized, undergone his temptation and called his disciples, he begins his ministry. In Mark, Jesus' ministry leads eventually to Jerusalem. It begins now in Galilee, specifically in Capernaum. Even though verses 14-16 describe the content of Jesus' proclamation, we can assume that this is Jesus' first sermon and that the earlier verses represent a summary of Jesus' message. Jesus begins his ministry by preaching in a synagogue. The narrator holds back many of the details about this event. We do not know how Jesus was invited to preach or even what he

20

said. The passage focuses our attention on the reaction to Jesus' message and the confrontation with the unclean spirit. This focus serves Mark's intention to connect Jesus' teaching with his actions of healing and exorcisms.

The scene contains three main characters: Jesus, the unclean spirit (the man possessed by the spirit is only a vessel and doesn't play a real role), and the congregants in the synagogue. The disciples are present, but do not act or speak. The scribes are mentioned, even though they are not present. The contrast between Jesus' teaching and that of the scribes foreshadows the conflict between Jesus and the Jewish leaders that develops later. Because the congregants act and speak as one, they represent only one character.

The congregants serve to help the reader understand the authority of Jesus' teaching. The narrator tells us that they were "astounded" at Jesus' teaching because he taught with "authority." The congregants themselves speak in verse 27. Their words link Jesus' teaching with his act of casting out the unclean spirit. The congregants serve to summarize the theology of the story.

What we know of Jesus in this story comes from what the narrator tells us, and Jesus' one line in verse 25. We know that Jesus taught and cast out an unclean spirit. We don't know how Jesus felt about encountering the unclean spirit or about his growing fame at the end of the story. Jesus largely remains a mystery to us in this story. The narrator's comment about Jesus' spreading fame foreshadows the crowds who will surround Jesus during his miracle-working ministry.

The most developed character in the story is the unclean spirit. We know something of his emotional state. He is afraid or at least apprehensive of Jesus, asking, "Have you come to destroy us?" (v. 24). He is the character in the story who is on a quest. He brings the fight to Jesus. He appears suddenly in the synagogue, confronting Jesus. In seeking Jesus out and calling him by name ("Jesus of Nazareth," v. 24), the unclean spirit is likely trying to vanquish Jesus. The unclean spirit knows that Jesus is the "Holy One of God" (v. 24). He believes that by calling Jesus' name he can gain control over Jesus, since knowing a divine being's name gave one a certain advantage over that divine being. Obviously, the unclean spirit's quest is a failed quest, as Jesus handily defeats him. The narrator adds to the drama of the story by telling us of the loud cry that the spirit makes when it leaves the man.

The plot of the story revolves around the conflict between Jesus and the unclean spirit. The suddenness of the spirit's appearance and his tough talk ("I know who you are,") make him appear to be a formidable opponent. Jesus defeats the unclean spirit with only a sentence. The spirit can offer no real resistance. We do not know what happens to the spirit once it leaves the man. We do not know if the loud cry is a death cry or only one of anguish at being vanquished. To the narrator, it is enough for us to know that Jesus easily defeated the spirit.

Theological Reflection

By placing this incident at the very beginning of Jesus' ministry, Mark indicates that a significant part of Jesus' mission is to purge the land of demonic forces (see Zechariah 13:2). Jesus performs the same ministry in Gentile territory in chapter 5 (the Gerasene demoniac). When Mark summarizes Jesus' ministry, exorcism or confrontation with unclean spirits is always a part of what Jesus does (see Mark 1:34; 3:11). The exorcism in Mark 9:14-27 highlights how difficult casting out unclean spirits is. That passage implies that, with enough faith, people can cast them out (see v. 19 and v. 29). In Mark 9:38, an unidentified exorcist is able to cast out demons in Jesus' name. Working outside the established "church," the exorcist can do what the disciples apparently cannot.

The role of demons in Mark raises theological questions about the creation. The book of Genesis affirms unequivocally that God's creation is good (Genesis 1:31, *passim*). The Gospel of John announces, "All things came into being through him" (John 1:3). Colossians 1:16 affirms that "all things in heaven and on earth were created, things visible and invisible, whether thrones or dominions or rulers or powers — all things have been created through him and for him (Christ)." These spiritual forces and power are part of God's good creation, even though they oppose God's will. As stated above, the role of Satan evolved within the Bible. Throughout most of the Old Testament, Satan was a member of God's heavenly host. Even though the popular belief exists today that Satan is a "fallen angel," the Bible never explains the origin of Satan and demons. (Isaiah 14:12-17, a poetic text, is not talking about Satan, but about foreign kings.) We do not know why they oppose God's will and torment human beings. Do they choose to be evil, or are they evil by nature? In the end, we are left with a mystery about creation — why the evil powers are part of God's good creation, and why evil is so prevalent and so strong.

The presence of unclean spirits also causes us to reflect on human responsibility for sinfulness. Even though Mark describes possession by unclean spirits, he does not portray these spirits as causing sin. The unclean spirits and demons cause bizarre and self-destructive behavior, but not the kind of disobedience that Satan causes in 1 Chronicles, or induces in Judas in John 13:27. Still, even though human beings are responsible for their own sins, the presence of unclean spirits indicates that human sinfulness is part of the fallen creation. We are caught up in a corruption bigger than we are. We are trapped by forces stronger than we are. We will not overcome evil only by our own effort. Only in the fullness of the dominion of God will we be free of sin.

The unclean spirit correctly identifies Jesus, "I know who you are, the Holy One of God." Even though the key christological term for Mark is "Son of God," the term used by the unclean spirit helps us understand Jesus' identity. By acknowledging that Jesus is the Holy One of God, the unclean spirit affirms Jesus' priestly function. Aaron, the priest, is called the "holy one of the Lord" in Psalm 106:16. Jesus is the intermediary between the people and God. The understanding of the word "holy" goes back to the Old Testament cultus and refers to the set apartness, or ritual cleanliness, of a person or object. The spirit contrasts Jesus with himself by calling him "holy." Ironically, the unclean spirit is correct about Jesus' identity and mission ("Have you come to destroy us?") The human characters in Mark are not so quick to catch on.

The passage twice refers to the authority of Jesus' teaching. The congregants even refer to the exorcism itself as a "teaching." These references communicate the authenticity of Jesus' teaching

23

and ministry, and to the congruity between Jesus' words and actions. The content of Jesus' teaching was that the dominion of God had come near. Jesus' actions manifested the reality of the in-breaking of the dominion of God.

Pastoral Reading
The preacher can help the congregation identify with this passage in at least two ways. In one sense, we are like the man with the unclean spirit. Along with the rest of creation we have been influenced by demonic forces. We know nothing about the man before he became the vehicle for the unclean spirit, but we know he was not himself. Neither are we. We do not know if the man was aware of his possession, but often we are not aware of the ways we have been corrupted by the demonic forces.

Another way we can identify with this passage is to connect Jesus' exorcism with the ministry of the church. In spite of our sinfulness, the risen Christ calls the church to continue the ministry of healing and opposition to the demonic. Just as Jesus faced a spiritual battle in his ministry, so the church faces a spiritual battle in its ministry in the world. Even if we don't believe in the actual existence of entities that can be called demons or unclean spirits, the evil of the world seems tenacious, intractable, and even cunning. Certainly, the evil of the world seems larger, more senseless and ferocious than humans should be capable of committing. Part of the ministry of the church is to oppose things in the world that seem demonic: racism, injustice, torture, oppression, addiction, hatred, exploitation, and a host of others. Even things we consider good, such as American military might, can be either demonic, or corrupted by demonic forces. These things seem demonic because they are so destructive and self-defeating. They serve no purpose and certainly oppose God's will for creation. They destroy people's lives and cause untold misery. Even if it is frustrating to do such battle, the church is called to be in conflict with these demonic forces. The implication of the exorcism story in Mark 9:17-31 is that the church can engage in this battle with faith and prayer. Just as Jesus' teachings and actions were congruent, so the church must

24

maintain integrity between word and deed, if we are to bear witness to a world suffering from, yet oblivious to, the demonic forces.

Part of reading this story in a pastoral way is to decide what we believe about the biblical understandings of demonology. Do we believe in entities that oppose God's will and can influence human behavior? Are these stories part of the outdated mythology of the ancient world? If such entities exist, can they not understand that they cannot win out over God? What is their purpose in opposing God's will and seeking to cause destruction and tragedy? What do they have against God and humanity? By what mechanism do they influence human behavior and other events? If it is incorrect to speak of the demonic as entities, how do we explain the evil of the world? Why do we, with no outside influence, act in such cruel, self-destructive, and foolish ways? Why can we not choose to be sinless if no outside influence acts upon us?

Whatever our answer to these questions, we know that evil seems defiant and stubborn. Evil steals innocence. We are too often influenced, if not controlled, by such things as addiction, mob mentality, and our own weaknesses and compulsions. Parents, relatives, and even church members pass on their prejudices. Desperation makes us do things we wouldn't ordinarily do. The evil of the world is more than just the collective sins of humanity. We are caught in a web of evil that distorts our souls, individually and corporately. The presence of the unclean spirit in a place of worship raises questions about the demonic even in the church. Many things in the church are liable to demonic influence: our use of money, our willingness to be co-opted by political parties, even our quest for success as defined by the world's standards. A spiritual dimension to sin exists, and the church is called to identify it and battle against it. Only God can ultimately win the battle, but the church keeps up the resistance, as an act of faithfulness to God, and for the sake of those hurt most by the world's evil.

Preaching Strategies

The preacher has two hurdles to overcome in preaching this text. The first is to enable the congregation to think theologically about the demonic. The second is to enable the congregation to see

25

how the risen Christ empowers the church's ministry against the demonic forces.

The challenge in helping a congregation reflect theologically about the demonic is that contemporary Christians in the mainline denominations do not take the demonic and cosmic dimension of evil seriously enough. The preacher certainly does not want to encourage any kind of simplistic belief in demons or demon possession. For example, people with mental illness are not "possessed." Yet, the existence of mental illness is an example of the fallen nature of the creation, of the demonic that seeks to corrupt God's good creation. We, as preachers, want to enable our congregations to see the demonic and spiritual dimension of evil. One strategy for doing that might be to lead the congregation to the recognition that evil seems to be more destructive, intractable, and senseless than human weakness could explain. Perhaps the preacher could enumerate examples of the terrible nature of evil: racism, cruelty, pointless nihilism, and self-defeating behavior. Once the congregation had an idea of how serious the problem of evil is, the preacher could move to a discussion of the biblical understanding of the demonic as the inexplicable corruption of God's good creation. As the Epistle to the Ephesians says, "For our struggle is not against enemies of blood and flesh, but against the rulers, against the authorities, against the cosmic powers of this present darkness, against the spiritual forces of evil in the heavenly places" (Ephesians 6:12).

For the second hurdle, the preacher could call the church to stand in opposition to the demonic forces in creation. In worship, proclamation, nurture, witness, outreach, and justice ministries, the church confronts the forces that seek to corrupt God's good creation. The risen Christ works within the church in these ministries. We do not see unclean spirits leave dramatically as in this passage, but we see the church's victories over the demonic forces in society. The preacher could give examples of how the church has successfully worked at reconciliation, the alleviation of suffering, reduction of violence, the reclaiming of lost lives. Each of these is a manifestation of God's victory through Christ over the demonic forces, and the coming near of the realm of God.

---

1. The parallel passage in 1 Samuel 24 uses the same Hebrew root for "incite," but attributes the inciting to the Lord (1 Samuel 24:1). In that passage, the Lord is angry at Israel.

Miracle Two

Enabling And Receiving Hospitality

The Text

As soon as they left the synagogue, they entered the house of Simon and Andrew, with James and John. Now Simon's mother-in-law was in bed with a fever, and they told him about her at once. He came and took her by the hand and lifted her up. Then the fever left her, and she began to serve them.

Jesus has already had a busy day. Vanquishing an unclean spirit right after preaching his first sermon should be enough for one sabbath. The need of the world, however, is too great for Jesus to rest. No sooner does he get back to the house where he is staying than he confronts more suffering. Simon's mother-in-law has a fever. This passage is quite brief, and written rather cryptically, but it teaches us some important things about Jesus and his ministry, and has generated much needed discussion about the role of women in Mark and the New Testament.

Background
The term "fever" is not mentioned much in the Old Testament. Two parallel texts describe fever as one of the punishments of the people of Israel if they do not obey the Lord's commandments and ordinances once they reach the promised land (Leviticus 26:16; Deuteronomy 28:22). Mark does not give the slightest hint that Simon's mother-in-law is being punished for disobedience. The emphasis in the passage is likely on the fever as a typical illness

that strikes people randomly. Such illnesses are part of general human suffering.

The New Testament contains a few other stories about the healing of fevers. Matthew and Luke have parallel accounts of this passage (Matthew 8:14-17 and Luke 4:38-41). John records an account of Jesus healing the son of a royal official, a Gentile. The boy is on the point of death, and one of his symptoms is a fever. Jesus heals the boy remotely, without having to touch him (John 4:46-54). In Acts, Paul heals the father of Publius, a citizen of Malta. Paul heals the man by prayer and laying on of hands (Acts 28:7-10).

In all likelihood, the fever the woman had resulted from malaria. Malaria was widespread in the Mediterranean in the first century. Malaria is caused by parasites carried by mosquitoes. Its symptoms include fever, chills, and weakness. It can be fatal.

Literary Analysis

This little incident is extraordinarily brief, even for Mark, and sparse in the details. No character speaks in the story; we learn all we know from the narrator. The story does not contain significant conflict. We do not know how long Simon's mother-in-law had been ill with the fever, or if the very reason why they go to Simon and Andrew's house is so that Jesus can heal her. It is possible the fever started that day and that Simon and Andrew did not know she was sick before they got to the house. We don't know how serious the fever was or whether she was close to death.

The characters in the story are Simon, Andrew, James, and John (the four disciples at this point), Jesus, and Simon's mother-in-law (who is unnamed). The narrator does not tell us exactly who informed Jesus that the woman is ill, only that "they" did. The narrator does not tell us the level of anxiety or urgency about the illness.

The lack of dialogue and details puts the focus on Jesus' actions to heal the woman. He "took her by the hand and lifted her up" (v. 31). The Greek text actually puts "he lifted her up" first, emphasizing Jesus' power. In Mark, Jesus' actions and words reinforce each other. Here the emphasis is on Jesus' actions. Jesus communicates the wholeness of the kingdom by his healing.

30

Even though this story is brief and lean, it adds much to our understanding of Jesus' ministry in Mark. To this point, Jesus has not yet healed anyone; he has only cast out an unclean spirit. Nevertheless, the four disciples (assuming that's who "they" are) tell Jesus about the woman's fever. They assume he can heal her. The disciples are the first to make the link between Jesus' exorcisms and his healing. The disciples are beginning to trust Jesus and respect his power. The story also shows Jesus' compassion in the tender way he treats the woman. By telling the reader that Jesus "lifted" the woman up, the narrator foreshadows Jesus' power over life and death, as well as Jesus' own resurrection. The crowds who come to be healed after sundown demonstrate the extent of the need in the town (and really in the world itself), and anticipate the crowds who follow Jesus during the early part of his ministry, when he acts as the healer.

Theological Reflection

Preachers ought not to misinterpret this illness. Even though the Old Testament background considers fever as one possible punishment for disobedience, the woman's fever is not treated in this passage as any kind of punishment, or as a result of her sinfulness. Jesus does not mention forgiveness. Even though this healing is sandwiched in between exorcisms, Mark does not portray fever as a result of demonic possession (but see the parallel text in Luke, where Jesus "rebukes" the fever, Luke 4:38-41). Mark does say that the fever "left" her, but this is slim evidence that the fever was caused by a demon.

This passage reflects the theological assumption that God's will for creation, including people, is health and wholeness. Illnesses, including fever, are part of the corruption of God's good creation. Human sinfulness did not cause the corruption of the creation, but human sinfulness magnifies it. As stated above, the Bible does not really give a full description of how and why God's good creation has been corrupted. The Bible simply affirms that the illness, grief, and suffering we experience in the world are not God's ultimate intention for creation. For the present, as Paul expresses it, the creation has been subjected to futility (Romans 8:20). As a

31

manifestation of the dominion of God coming near, Jesus restores the woman to soundness of body.

Pastoral Reading

By telling Jesus about the woman's fever, the disciples remind us of how anxious we are, and how helpless we feel when a loved one is sick. Most churches keep a prayer list of people in the congregation and the wider community who are ill, facing surgery, or have some health problem. Watching a loved one who truly is in pain and suffering can be agony.

The scene in verses 32-34, where the whole town brings people who are ill or who have a demon speaks to the sheer magnitude of the world's need. Mark seems to exaggerate when he declares, "the whole city was gathered around the door" (v. 33). Churches constantly receive appeals for money and volunteers to meet some need. Just as Jesus healed "many" on that sabbath night, so the church must combat "compassion fatigue" in helping to alleviate suffering. No one congregation can meet every need, but the church as a whole is called to stretch its resources, and respond, even when we are tired and it looks as if the checkbook is drained.

Malaria is a severe problem in many parts of the world. In climates hospitable for the proliferation of mosquitoes, such as that of sub-Sahara Africa, malaria is endemic. The disease is becoming resistant to the drugs that have been used to fight it. Part of the ministry of the church is to provide medical missionaries who treat and prevent illnesses such as malaria and palliative care for those who cannot be cured.

A significant aspect of interpreting this passage is to determine what the text will allow us to say about the role of women in ministry. Verse 31 tells us that after the woman was cured of her fever, "she began to serve them." As others have noted, at least part of the reason Mark tells us this detail is to confirm the completeness of the cure. She did not lie in bed weak from the aftereffects of the fever, but was well enough to get up and perform her household duties.

On the one hand, the reference to her service seems to reinforce stereotypical roles for women. As some women have quipped,

Jesus healed her just in time for supper! Everyone is familiar with the image of the harried wife and mother who has to keep going even when she is sick. Is Mark buying in to that image? Certainly, Mark does not challenge the traditional assumption that Simon's mother-in-law was responsible for hospitality in the home. We assume that her "service" was overseeing a meal. Servants or younger women may have done the actual preparation of the food. Nevertheless, the service was likely the rather unglamorous domestic work often done by women.

Mark cannot easily be dismissed, however, as one who denigrates the role of women. In verses 32-34, Jesus himself serves those who have come to the house, even though we would expect him to be tired. The Greek word used for the woman's service is the same word used of the angels who "waited on" Jesus during his wilderness temptation (1:13). One of the defining statements in the Gospel of Mark for Jesus' purpose is found in 10:45 — "For the Son of Man came not to be served but to serve, and to give his life a ransom for many." In the two preceding verses, Jesus declares that those who are great or first among us are the ones who act as servant (same Greek root as the woman's service) and slave. Although it is true that neither Jesus nor Mark challenged the traditional roles of women, as moderns would have appreciated, Jesus calls all disciples to service and models that service. Service is the path to greatness for all disciples.

Preaching Strategies

A sermon from this text might revolve around the theological dynamic in the passage between trust in Jesus and service. The disciples display trust in Jesus by telling him about Simon's mother-in-law. They assume both that Jesus can heal her and that he will. Their instinct is to turn to Jesus in a time of need. The townspeople also trust Jesus by coming at sundown (when sabbath is over) to be healed and purged of demons.

In contemporary situations, this sense of trust is not automatic. We have trouble trusting in God and the risen Christ in times of trouble, illness, or tragedy. All pastors are asked to pray for people in need. Many times when people have asked me to pray for them, they either have said explicitly, or I have inferred from their tone of voice, that they thought my prayer would "get through," because I am an ordained minister. They did not assume that God would hear their prayers. Many experiences can undermine our trust in God. If we do not see concrete "cures" of illnesses, we often wonder if God hears our prayers. This passage gives the preacher an opportunity to address the issue of trust in God.

This passage affirms a strong call to service. Simon's mother-in-law serves those in her house after she is cured. Her service is a spontaneous response to the grace Jesus has shown her in her healing. The preacher ought to adopt some rhetorical strategy to reinforce the idea that men and women can serve equally well in all areas of the church's ministry. Jesus serves those who come in droves to the house after sunset. The church, which is called to carry on the ministry of Jesus, models that commitment to service.

The preacher could point to specific ministries in the community where the church could carry out this call to service. The preacher can acknowledge the magnitude of the need and proclaim that God strengthens us for the service to which we are called.

Miracle Three

Begging, Touching, Healing, Growling

The Text

A leper came to him begging him, and kneeling he said to him, "If you choose, you can make me clean." Moved by pity, Jesus stretched out his hand and touched him, and said to him, "I do choose. Be made clean!" Immediately the leprosy left him, and he was made clean. After sternly warning him he sent him away at once, saying to him, "See that you say nothing to anyone; but go, show yourself to the priest, and offer for your cleansing what Moses commanded, as a testimony to them." But he went out and began to proclaim it freely, and to spread the word, so that Jesus could no longer go into a town openly, but stayed out in the country; and people came to him from every quarter.

Jesus' ministry is now all of two days old. Following his dramatic and potentially exhausting sabbath day, Jesus arises early the next day for prayer. The disciples inform him "Everyone (presumably the crowds of sick and demon-possessed) is searching for you." Jesus' work is not going to slow down! Jesus goes into the smaller towns around Capernaum (an inspiration for town and country pastors) to preach. The summary of Jesus' ministry in verse 39 includes preaching and exorcism, but not specifically healing.

Jesus' ministry in the countryside of Galilee is the setting for the healing in this passage, although the narrative does not include a time reference. Because Mark does not tell us that the healing of the leper happened on the day after the synagogue incident, the exact timing likely doesn't matter. The story itself helps us sharpen our understanding of Jesus' healing ministry. The account has many puzzling features, including some difficult choices to make in translation. We get more details than we did in the account of the healing of Simon's mother-in-law, but those details serve almost to make the story more difficult to interpret.

Background

Medical historians have reached a consensus that the leprosy mentioned in the Bible is not the Hansen's disease now known as leprosy. The leprosy in the Bible is a broad term including many different skin ailments, such as eczema, psoriasis, and seborrhea. Some of the skin conditions described in the Old Testament purity laws cannot be identified by contemporary science. These conditions caused great discomfort, but were not life threatening. Even though, historically, the conditions in the Bible are not true leprosy, in this discussion, I will refer to lepers and leprosy for the biblical accounts.[1]

As is well known, in the Old Testament people with skin diseases were considered unclean and were required to isolate themselves. This "uncleanness" was a ritual uncleanness and prevented the person from taking part in the religious life of the community. Leviticus 13-14 contains extensive instructions about the identification (one might say diagnosis) of the various skin ailments and treatment, and about the requirements for the person to be declared clean and returned to community life. The restrictions on people with skin diseases are especially poignant.

"The person who has the leprous disease shall wear torn clothes and let the hair of his head be disheveled; and he shall cover his upper lip and cry out, 'Unclean, unclean.' He shall remain unclean as long as he has the disease; he is unclean. He shall live alone; his dwelling shall be outside the camp" (Leviticus 13:45-46).

As in the previous chapter, concerning fevers, leprosy in the Old Testament was often considered a punishment for sin. In Numbers 12, Miriam and Aaron criticize Moses because he married a Cushite woman. They boast that God speaks through them as well

36

as through Moses. The Lord is angry with Aaron and Miriam and punishes Miriam with a condition that the narrator calls leprosy. Miriam's symptom is that her skin turns white. Aaron interprets her condition as a punishment and intervenes with the Lord on her behalf. Miriam is quarantined, and the people cannot continue their journey until she is clean again.

The story of Naaman in 2 Kings 5 demonstrates the Lord's grace and the assumption that leprosy was considered a punishment. Naaman, an officer in the Aramean army — an enemy of Israel — is a successful soldier but also a leper. An Israelite slave girl tells him to consult Elisha. Naaman reluctantly follows Elisha's advice to submerge himself in the Jordan River, but is healed of his leprosy when he does. This part of the story shows God's grace to a foreigner, one who is even hostile to Israel, the chosen people. (See Luke 4:27 for a New Testament interpretation of this story.) Gehazi, Elisha's assistant, decides to make a profit off of the healing, and deceitfully persuades Naaman to give him money. Elisha punishes Gehazi with leprosy.

Uzziah, the king of Israel, was also struck with leprosy as a punishment (2 Chronicles 26:16-21). Uzziah (called Amaziah in 2 Kings) was an ambiguous king. He did many good things, such as removing the "high places" used for idolatrous sacrifices, and making military and agricultural advancements. He also was impulsive and arrogant, and that led to his punishment with leprosy. Full of himself with his successes, he entered the temple to make an offering on the altar, which only priests were permitted to do. When confronted by the priests, Uzziah became angry. His anger and arrogance were punished with leprosy. The disease lasted the rest of his life, and he was forced to live in isolation, unable to enter the temple. His son, Jotham, ruled in his stead.

Literary Analysis

Before one can even begin to analyze this passage as a narrative, one must solve several problems of translation. These problems greatly affect how we understand the passage. The first of these matters is whether to include the word "kneeling" in verse 40 (see the footnote in the NRSV). If the leper did indeed kneel, he showed a posture of worship to Jesus. The manuscript evidence is mixed, but the use of the word is consistent with Mark's portrayal of people at this stage of his ministry. While Jesus is in "healing mode," people flock to him and treat him with respect.

The most serious translation problem in the passage is Jesus' initial emotional response to the leper's request. Some manuscripts say that Jesus is "moved with pity" toward the man (the position of the NRSV), while others say that Jesus is angry. Even today, translators are divided about how to translate the verse. I tend to agree with the translators who take the "angry" position. It is difficult to see why a scribe would have changed "pity" to "anger," but the reverse (changing anger to pity) is much more plausible. As will be discussed below, Jesus is not necessarily angry with the man.

Finally, in verse 43, Jesus "sternly warns" the man before sending him out (NRSV). The word for "sternly warn" is actually a Greek word that means to "growl" or "snort." This could be a further indication of Jesus' anger. It could also be a vestige from what originally was an exorcism account. We will explore below the implications of the connection between healing and demonic forces.

As a narrative, this account is quite dramatic, with more dialogue and intriguing developments than the account of the healing of Simon's mother-in-law. We don't know exactly when this incident took place, except that it was during Jesus' ministry in the Galilean countryside near Capernaum. Moving from verse 39 to verse 40, we go from the general to the specific. (The story in Mark's source may have originally had a different setting.)

The only two characters on stage are the leper and Jesus. The leper takes the initiative in approaching Jesus. His humble and respectful stance toward Jesus elicits our sympathy, as does his courage in approaching Jesus. We do not know what lies behind the leper's tentativeness in asking Jesus to heal him ("If you choose"). The leper's words assume that Jesus has the ability to heal; the question seems to be Jesus' willingness. Has Jesus given any indication of being selective in healing? Does the leper feel unworthy? Is he simply being polite? The answer may influence how we understand Jesus' anger in verse 41. Assuming that Jesus is not angry with the leper himself (for bothering him, or for implying that he healed selectively), with whom or what is Jesus angry? Is Jesus angry that the need is so great? Is Jesus angry that the isolation resulting from the purity laws has caused the man to devalue himself? (The Bible is not as concerned about "self-esteem" as we are.) The fact that Jesus violates the purity laws by touching the man suggests that perhaps he regarded them or their execution as oppressive. Jesus famously considered people's needs to be more important than the practice of the Sabbath laws. Whatever the focus of Jesus' anger, the reader of Mark gets some glimpse of Jesus' emotions and knows that the suffering of the world moves him to passion. Jesus' words and actions are congruent as he stretches out his hand (a detail that draws attention to Jesus' touch of the unclean leper), touches the man and then pronounces him clean.

After the healing itself, the story takes a curious turn. According to the Greek, Jesus "growls," and tells the man not to report the healing to anyone. Jesus instructs the man to go to the priests so that he can follow the prescribed cleansing ritual of the Mosaic Law. The NRSV interprets the growl as adding sternness to Jesus' warning about not reporting the healing to anyone. As suggested above, the growl may be the vestige of an exorcism story. More about that below. Despite everything — Jesus' compassion and possible sternness — the man does the exact opposite of what Jesus asks him to do. The character with whom we were so sympathetic at the beginning of the story lets Jesus down. The man's disobedience introduces the "messianic secret" in Mark. Jesus frequently tells people to keep quiet about his healings (see below). His disobedience also foreshadows the failure of every human character to understand and obey Jesus throughout the Gospel of Mark. Only at the crucifixion does the Centurion recognize Jesus as the Son of God. Even after the resurrection, the disciples are filled with fear.

By the end of the story, Jesus cannot go into the urban areas but must stay in the country to avoid the crowds. As the story progresses, the crowds become a frequent character in the narratives. This story highlights how Jesus is forced to adapt his ministry because of human foibles. At the end of the day on that first Sabbath, Jesus had to continue his healing ministry even after a trying day. Jesus' prayer time is interrupted the next day by the disciples looking for him. Now, Jesus must change his itinerary because the leper disobeyed him, leading to a crush of humanity in the urban areas.

Theological Reflection

Mark seems to make a distinction between healings and exorcisms. The man with the unclean spirit in 1:23 did not have an illness, and no symptoms were described. The summary of Jesus' ministry in 1:32-34 seems to differentiate between healing the sick and casting out demons. Nevertheless, the fact that the two are mentioned together so often is suggestive. Also, both the healing of Simon's mother-in-law and the healing of the leper contain some of the language of exorcism. The fever "left" Simon's mother-in-law. The leprosy "left" the man. Jesus "growled" after the exorcism. We should be careful in our interpretation of this connection. To Mark, the suffering, problems, and diseases of the world represent the demonic corruption of God's creation. The demonic can be an entity, as in 1:23ff, or it can be an inanimate illness, such as fever or leprosy. A responsible preacher would not say that every sick person has a "demon." Nevertheless, illness and impairment oppose God's will for the creation, and are, in that sense, demonic. We affirm the spiritual dimension to illness when we pray for the sick.

Mark emphasizes Jesus' touching the man. Touching a leper was considered a violation of Old Testament regulations. By touching the man, Jesus assumes a priestly authority to interpret the law. The goal of the law in both Judaism and Christianity is the proper ordering of communal and individual life. By touching the man, Jesus affirms that the law is life giving and reconciling.

Jesus' admonition to the man to "say nothing to anyone" is a classic example of what New Testament scholars call the "messianic secret." At times within the Gospel of Mark (and in Matthew and Luke), Jesus tells a person who has been healed to refrain from telling others of the healing. Also, Jesus tells the demons to keep quiet about his identity (see Mark 5:43 and 3:12; Matthew 12:6; Luke 4:41). Jesus' admonition to reticence is curious. One might assume that he is simply weary of the crowds, but they are already

40

around him. One more report won't make that much difference. The most plausible explanation has been that the "messianic secret" is a literary device that makes an important theological point. Mark has Jesus seek to hide his identity as a healer and exorcist because Mark does not want people to overemphasize the miraculous to the exclusion of service, discipleship, and taking up the cross. By having Jesus tell the demons and those who were healed to keep his identity secret, Mark is hinting that we cannot really understand Jesus fully at this point in the gospel. Only when the reader confronts the cross and the call to take up our own cross can we understand Jesus fully. The healings are God's gift to the world and the manifestation of the coming near of the dominion of God. Nevertheless, those healings do not prevent the cross, but even contribute to the call for Jesus' death. Mark warns us away from accepting the gifts of grace and healing without fully understanding our call to take up our cross and follow Jesus.

The former leper's disobedience also instructs us theologically. As we have said before, the human characters in Mark do not fully understand Jesus. Jesus' opponents fail and the disciples fail. Even at the end of the gospel, the disciples are silent and afraid. God uses the disciples in spite of their failure. Here in this passage the man spreads the "word," a term in Mark for the proclamation of the good news (see 2:2). God's purposes prevail, in spite of human failure.

Pastoral Reading
Every pastor is familiar with people who are only too eager to ask for help. Expecting an inordinate amount of the pastor's time, they call constantly, drop by unannounced (either at the parsonage or the office) and just generally wear their neediness on their sleeves. This passage points out the other side of the coin: people who need help, but are reluctant to ask. If the leper's opening phrase to Jesus ("If you choose") reflects anxiety or any sense of unworthiness for healing, then the leper reminds us of those people. We must communicate that God's grace is open to all people, even society's outcasts. The more pastors can be in the community (a difficult task these days), and communicate availability, the more the ones who

41

need help might be willing to come in. We have to set limits for the others.

The leper's problem was not just the discomfort of his skin condition, but his isolation from the community. Even Mark identifies him by his condition, and by no other characteristic. He was labeled unclean and had to shoo people away from himself. Researchers have discovered that social rejection is indeed physically painful. According to Naomi Eisenberger, "The shock and distress of this rejection (registers) in the same part of the brain, called the anterior cingulated cortex, that also responds to physical pain."[2] Our preaching — and our entire ministry — should speak to broken hearts and loneliness.

The passage calls us to reflect on how we regard our skin. Our skin seems to matter to us more than we think. People tan or bleach their skin to make themselves more attractive. We separate ourselves based on skin color. A tattoo or body piercing can be a sign of rebellion, conformity, solidarity, or all three for different circles. Social scientists know that skin diseases are the basis for exclusion in many cultures. This passage raises the question of whether the way we divide ourselves based on our skin reflects a healthy Christian attitude.

Many people have commented on the similarities between lepers of Jesus' day and AIDS patients of today. That connection can still be made and should not be neglected. Just as the leper was the object of Jesus' care and compassion, including touch, so AIDS patients should be treated with care and concern and made to feel as welcome and comfortable as possible. The AIDS epidemic is on a devastating rampage within Africa, of course, and Western nations should seek to provide education to prevent the disease, and drugs to fight it.

Preaching Strategies

This passage presents at least three themes that deserve attention in preaching. The first is Jesus' acceptance of an outcast. The second is Jesus' passion about the man's condition. The third is God's use of the man's testimony.

Both Jesus and the man seem to violate the ritual purity laws of the Old Testament. The leper came to Jesus (although we do not know how close he got), even though he should have warned Jesus away from himself. As is often the case in the gospel healing stories, the man has nothing to lose by asking for Jesus' healing. Possibly, his life could not have gotten much worse. Almost certainly he was in pain and discomfort; absolutely he was lonely and isolated. In contrast, Jesus has much to lose by coming in contact with the man. Contact with a leper would render Jesus ritually unclean. Nevertheless, Jesus does not upbraid the man or chase him away. Even though Jesus does not need to touch him in order to heal him (see 3:5 as one of many examples of Jesus healing someone without touch), he does just that. Are we reading too much into the narrative to say that Jesus heals both his loneliness and his leprosy by touching him? The preacher could cite numerous examples of contemporary situations in which people feel isolated, lonely, or unwelcome. People with certain diseases, or social phobias are often isolated. People of Middle Eastern descent, or immigrants, in general, often feel unwelcome in the United States. Part of the way the church continues Jesus' ministry is to reach out to those who have been rejected.

Verse 41 is so ambiguous that one must be careful in using it for proclamation. That ambiguity is such a pity, because the verse is so powerful. Mark gives us a glimpse into Jesus' feelings, but we aren't quite sure which feeling! Is Jesus moved to pity because of the man's suffering? Is he angry that the demonic forces have the man under their control? Is Jesus angry that the legal tradition has left the man isolated? We can't answer these questions with any certainty. A precise answer would enhance our preaching. What we can affirm is that Jesus was passionate about the healing. That Jesus feels strong emotion about our situation is reassuring. Jesus is affected by the world's suffering. Even in the midst of crowds of people needing ministry (1:24), Jesus is moved by the man's plight.

After all that Jesus has done for the man, he still disobeys Jesus. Jesus tells him to go the priests, but he goes out preaching instead. As Mark puts it, he "spread the word," a technical term for proclamation. Throughout the Gospel of Mark, the disciples and other followers of Jesus always manage to do the wrong thing. Nevertheless, God's purposes prevail. God can incorporate our mistakes into God's purposes.

---

1. See the article by David P. Wright and Richard N. Jones in David Noel Freedman, ed. *The Anchor Bible Dictionary* (New York: Doubleday, 1992), s.v. "Leprosy."

2. AOL news 10/9/03.

Miracle Four

Forgiveness
Starts A Fight

The Text

*When he returned to Capernaum after some days, it
was reported that he was at home. So many gathered
around that there was no longer room for them, not
even in front of the door; and he was speaking the word
to them. Then some people came, bringing to him a
paralyzed man, carried by four of them. And when they
could not bring him to Jesus because of the crowd, they
removed the roof above him; and after having dug
through it, they let down the mat on which the paralytic
lay. When Jesus saw their faith, he said to the paralytic, "Son, your sins are forgiven." Now some of the
scribes were sitting there, questioning in their hearts,
"Why does this fellow speak in this way? It is blas-
phemy! Who can forgive sins but God alone?" At once
Jesus perceived in his spirit that they were discussing
these questions among themselves; and he said to them,
"Why do you raise such questions in your hearts? Which
is easier, to say to the paralytic, 'Your sins are forgiven,'
or to say, 'Stand up and take your mat and walk'? But
so that you may know that the Son of Man has authority on earth to forgive sins" — he said to the paralytic
— "I say to you, stand up, take your mat and go to your
home." And he stood up, and immediately took the mat
and went out before all of them; so that they were all
amazed and glorified God, saying, "We have never seen
anything like this!"*

Beginning at chapter 2, Jesus' ministry takes a turn. To this point, Jesus has attracted crowds and built a reputation as a healer, exorcist, and wonder-worker. The only resistance to Jesus' ministry has come from demons, but that has been no contest. Jesus vanquishes demons without breaking a sweat. Now, he begins to encounter conflict from flesh and blood people, the religious officials. Mark has hinted at the roots of this conflict in the arrest of John the Baptist (1:14) and the comparison of Jesus to the scribes (1:22). Now that underlying conflict begins to build. Jesus continues as a miracle worker, but now he ministers under a cloud.

The passage in 2:1-12 is a hybrid story. When Jesus begins to offer more than physical healing, he runs afoul of the officials of his own people. This passage is both a healing story and a conflict story. The conflict is caused not by Jesus' healing, but by the offer of forgiveness. Some commentators believe that the original story was only what is in 2:1-5, 11-12, and that the conflict part of the story was added later. We will discuss this possibility below. In any case, the story as it stands makes a coherent and interesting narrative, raising many theological and pastoral issues.

Background

The paralyzed man in the story has two problems: he can't use his body, and his sins have not been forgiven (or possibly he does not realize that they have been forgiven). The Old Testament has much material to help us understand both of these needs. The Old Testament writers knew how important our bodies are, and how serious our sins can be.

The Old Testament writers did not extol the human body the way Greek artists did, with their many muscular and voluptuous statues. Nevertheless, they affirmed the human body as part of God's good creation. In the creation account in Genesis 2, the Lord God forms the first human out of dust with the divine fingers. The use of dust as material indicates the transitory nature of the human body, but God's care in shaping the body indicates the significance of the body. When the author of Genesis 2 reports about the Lord God breathing life into the dust, he affirms the unity of human embodiment (verse 7). The biblical writers would not support our common assumption about the division between "body" and "soul." People are unitary beings with body and soul inseparable.

A healthy, fully functioning body enabled a person to enjoy God's creation, and to do his or her part in God's directive to care for the creation (Genesis 1:29; 2:15). A healthy body enabled a person to participate in sex, both for enjoyment and for fulfilling God's command to populate the earth (Genesis 1:28). The Song of Solomon is a poetic celebration of the loving physical enjoyment of the body in sex. To be able to work led to a sense of fulfillment and productivity that earned prosperity and satisfaction. As the sages of Israel put it, "In all toil there is profit" (Proverbs 14:23). Several proverbs speak of the satisfaction and prosperity that derive from work. The value of work is contrasted with the plight of the lazy. Because the part of the proverbs that chastise the lazy does not apply to the situation of one who is paralyzed, we should look only at the half of the proverb that extols the virtues and rewards of work. "The hand of the diligent makes rich" (Proverbs 10:4b). In the biblical worldview, a person whose body will not function misses out on the rewards of work and on the engagement with God's creation.

2 Samuel contains the brief story of Mephibosheth, the grandson of Saul and the son of Jonathan, David's companion. Mephibosheth's nurse dropped him when he was five years old, crippling both of his feet. We don't know much about Mephibosheth, but David took care of him after the death of Jonathan. We might infer that he could not work from 2 Samuel 9:10, but he did have a son. In talking to King David, Mephibosheth refers to himself as a "dead dog," a self-deprecatory term that may refer to his physical condition or perhaps to his political situation, now that the kingship has passed to David. Even though Mephibosheth was not paralyzed, his story sheds some light on the dependency and perhaps low self-esteem of those who cannot walk well (2 Samuel 4:4; 9:6-13; 16:1-4; 19:24-30).

Because of advances in medical technology, paralysis is a much more common condition today than in biblical times. Today people can survive falls, automobile accidents, skiing mishaps, and head injuries, all of which can cause paralysis. In the biblical world, a fall or diving accident, which could cause paralysis, would likely kill the victim. I do not have good information about strokes in the biblical world. Perhaps the paralysis of the man in Mark 2 was caused by polio.

Jesus also forgives the man's sins. The biblical understanding of sin and forgiveness is complex. Several metaphors help shape these understandings. Sin is a debt we cannot pay, a mark we miss, a power from which we cannot free ourselves, a boundary we cross, or a commandment we disobey. The Old Testament knows the whole panoply of sins: greed, lust, arrogance, disobedience, idolatry, and selfishness, among others. Sin is a universal human problem (Psalm 14:3), and can be individual or collective. The prophets often admonish the whole community for sins of greed and injustice (Amos 2:4-8). Forgiveness is God's grace to repair the damage sin does. Forgiveness is repaying our debt, restoring our place, releasing our bonds, and absolving our disobedience.

Leviticus 4-7 gives instructions about how the priests were to perform the sacrifices for atonement for sin. Personal confession of sin was part of the process for forgiveness (Leviticus 5:5). The prophets taught that showing mercy was a proper response to sin and was what God wanted more than sacrifice (Hosea 6:6). Although the priests served as mediators between the people and God, true forgiveness came from God.

The Old Testament contains several prayers of confession that help us understand how the people understood sin and how they expressed of contrition. Psalm 51 is a poignant outpouring of guilt and a heartfelt plea for forgiveness. The psalmist asks that God take away his guilt (v. 7) and change him from within (v. 10). He wants again to know the presence of God's spirit (v. 11). Ezra 9, Nehemiah 9, and Daniel 9 all contain communal prayers of confession offered on behalf of the whole people. These three prayers acknowledge that the people have disobeyed God, in spite of God's providence on their behalf. The prayers all assume that forgiveness is possible only because God is merciful (Ezra 9:8-9; Nehemiah 9:31; Daniel 9:17-19).

Although Mark does not at all imply that the man's paralysis is a punishment for sin or was caused by excessive guilt, the writer of Psalm 32 recognized a connection between guilt and physical sickness. The psalmist asserts that his refusal to confess his sins contributed to a physical illness. "While I kept silence, my body wasted away through my groaning all day long" (Psalm 32:3). Confession of his sin and the knowledge of forgiveness contributed to his recovery (v. 5).

Some Old Testament texts refer to care for or recovery of the lame as a sign of God's favor. Isaiah 35:6 says that, "then the lame shall leap like a deer." Micah paints a beautiful picture of an eschatological vision of God's grace. Part of that vision is that the Lord will "assemble the lame" (Micah 4:6). These verses reflect God's concern for, and promise of, eschatological healing for those whose legs and bodies do not function well (see also Jeremiah 31:8 and Zephaniah 3:19).

Literary Analysis

As noted above, many New Testament scholars consider this to be a composite story. The original story did not contain the conflict with the scribes in verses 6-10. In all likelihood, this section was written later and added to the original story. This suggestion is supported by the lack of response from the scribes in verse 12. If this hypothesis about the original story is accurate, the story in its earlier form suggests a stronger connection between the forgiveness of the man's sins and his healing. Jesus' words to the man would have been, "Son, your sins are forgiven. I say to you, stand up, take your mat and go to your home." This version would have been ambiguous about whether the forgiveness effected the healing. In any case, in the account we have now, the preacher must deal with a complicated story in which the themes of healing, forgiveness, and the authority of Jesus are interwoven. In our discussion below, we will treat the story as we have it, as one story.

As the narrative opens, Jesus has returned to Capernaum, even though he had retreated to the countryside in chapter 1. Once again, the crowds surround Jesus. The narrator adds the detail that there is not enough room for everyone. Jesus is boxed into the house

(Simon's house again?). The presence of the crowds communicates Jesus' popularity at this point in his ministry and sets up the event that demonstrates the faith of the four men who carry their friend. At the end of the story, the exclamation of the crowd — "We have never seen anything like this!" — helps the reader to understand the uniqueness of Jesus' ministry.

This story is driven more by plot than by characterization. The paralytic never speaks, nor do his friends. The action of the friends in bringing the man to Jesus and devising a way to get him to Jesus is endearing and shows some daring. The scribes discuss theology and do not reveal much about themselves. Most of their dialogue is in the form of rhetorical questions. Even Jesus largely engages in argument with the scribes, again asking rhetorical questions. His initial comment to the paralytic, "Son, your sins are forgiven," shows Jesus' compassion, but that is not much in the way of character development. The resolution of the conflict between Jesus and the scribes makes the story work.

The conflict arises because Jesus adds something to the healing. Although Jesus has called his hearers to repent (1:15), he has not at this point pronounced forgiveness for anyone. Presumably, if Jesus had simply healed the man, the conflict would never have arisen. The scribes object to Jesus telling the man his sins are forgiven. We might note that the objection of the scribes has merit. It is God's prerogative to show mercy and forgive sins. Jesus' offer of forgiveness is abrupt both because this is the initial mention of forgiveness in Mark and because we presume that the four men did not bring their companion to Jesus for forgiveness. To this point, Jesus has shown his power in healing and exorcism. Perhaps the four men assume, as did the scribes, that Jesus does not forgive sins. Although the text does not explicitly say so, the four men likely wanted Jesus to heal the man's paralysis. The abrupt introduction of forgiveness focuses our attention. Mark is telling us something important about forgiveness. Marks' literary device of abruptly introducing forgiveness and combining forgiveness with healing makes a theological point. Both paralysis and the power of sin are examples of the fallen nature of the creation. The coming near of the dominion of God manifests itself in physical healing and release from the demonic power of sin. By combining healing and forgiveness in one narrative, Mark reveals how thoroughly we are subjected to the demonic powers and how complete is Jesus' ministry in releasing us.

In the dialogue with the scribes, Jesus' argument seems to be that if he has the power to heal the man, he therefore has the authority to forgive sins. The healing has a dual purpose: it is an act of compassion that manifests the coming near of the dominion of God, and it helps the reader to identify Jesus as one authorized to forgive sins. The completeness of the healing is demonstrated when the man picks up his mat and walks away. (Is there now more room to move about among the crowds?) As stated above, we do not know whether the scribes were convinced about Jesus' authority to forgive sins. The narrator does not tell us, unless the "all" in verse 12 includes them, an unlikely supposition. To the crowds, at least, the healing has resolved the conflict.

Theological Reflection

The primary theological issue in the passage is the identity of Jesus. In chapter 1, Jesus has amply demonstrated that he has the power to heal and vanquish demonic forces. This passage ups the ante. We will learn that Jesus is more than a healer and exorcist, of which there were many reports (see 9:38). The scribes themselves raise the theological question, "Who can forgive sins but God alone?" (v. 7). The question of the scribes pushes the reader to make the conclusion that Jesus is a divine being. The title Jesus uses of himself is "Son of Man." This term had a long history, beginning with Daniel 7:13-14. In Daniel, the *one like a human being* is a heavenly being who shares authority with God (the Ancient One). Such an idea is unique in the Old Testament. In the intertestamental period, the term, Son of Man, became a title, and began to take on messianic qualities. Jesus may be saying that his ministry is a fulfillment of Old Testament prophecies, such as Isaiah 35 (see above), and that as the Messiah he has authority to forgive sins. Just as the figure of the *one like a human being* in Daniel 7 represents release from both Greek rule and the cosmic powers of the four beasts, so in Jesus the creation is released from demonic

51

power. That demonic power is manifested both in physical limitations and in the power of sin.

Another important theological issue in the passage is the understanding of faith. The miracle stories in the gospels help us to add nuance to our understanding of faith. This is the first of the healing stories in which anyone's faith is mentioned (by the narrator in this case). The reader must discern from the actions of the four men what they contribute to our understanding of faith. Throughout the Gospel of Mark, faith is trust and confidence in Jesus. This narrative shows how the four men act upon their trust and confidence. The very act of bringing the man to Jesus shows compassion, but that may well be a component of faith. The really dramatic action of the men is to dig through the roof to lower their friend to Jesus. This action shows tenacity, daring, and some ingenuity. The four men refuse to let obstacles get in their way. Having faith does not seem to mean that the men had a deep theological understanding of who Jesus really was. The narrator gives us no inkling that they recognized Jesus as the Messiah. Concern for their friend and dogged determination seem to be the components of their faith.

The passage highlights the connection between physical healing and forgiveness. The man is physically healed of his paralysis, but is also forgiven. Psalm 103 makes this connection. Verse 3 extols the Lord as one who "forgives all your iniquity and heals all your diseases." Sometimes, commentators assert that Jesus heals the man by forgiving his sins. The text is clear that these are two separate actions. The man does not get up and walk until after Jesus has the conversation with the scribes and tells the man to get up. This separation indicates that the man's paralysis was not psychosomatic. He was not paralyzed because of his guilt over his sins. Even if the healing and forgiveness are separate actions in the text, they are connected theologically. Both are examples of Jesus' power to release people from the demonic powers.

Pastoral Reading
Will Willimon, a United Methodist Bishop, has said many times that pastors and churches think they exist to "meet people's needs."

Willimon's response to that assumption is to declare that sometimes the gospel gives us needs we didn't know we had. This passage seems to be a perfect example of Willimon's insight. Surely, the four men did not dig through the roof of the house so that the man could have his sins forgiven! They wanted their friend healed of his paralysis. They thought they knew his need. Jesus perceived a need they didn't think about. The man's sins had not been forgiven. Did Jesus think the men had carried him and dug through the roof so that Jesus would forgive him? Would Jesus also have healed him if not for the complaints of the scribes? In any case, Jesus recognized the need no one else saw. We often bring a single complaint to God when our real need is more comprehensive. We want one thing healed; God offers total transformation.

The passage raises the question of whether we recognize our need for forgiveness. We bring many concerns to God in prayer. Most churches have prayer lists and some way of taking prayer requests during worship. How often do these prayer requests ask for forgiveness? We should take our need for forgiveness as seriously as we take our other prayer requests.

The action of the four men highlights the accessibility of Jesus and, hence, of God. Every pastor has counseled people who thought God wouldn't bother with their prayers. The four men are so intent on getting their friend to Jesus that they break in line ahead of the crowds around Jesus. Mark doesn't tell us whether anyone else in the crowd had come for healing. Every other passage indicates that wherever Jesus goes, the crowds come at least in part for healing and exorcism. The passage leaves open the possibility that others there wanted to be healed. One wonders what the crowd thought of these four men who took their friend to the head of the line. The rest of the crowd seemed content to wait their turn. In any case, the four men tear up a roof and interrupt Jesus' sermon to get their friend to him. Persistence and maybe even pushiness in taking our needs to God, seem to be components of faith.

The passage raises the issue of the experience of being forgiven. Most of us would consider healing a paralyzed person to be more difficult than pronouncing forgiveness for sins. On the one hand, many people are not able either to forgive themselves or to accept God's forgiveness. Many times, people in pastoral counseling situations have told me that their sins were too bad for God to forgive. Enabling people genuinely to experience the forgiveness God offers is not easy. Not only the reality of forgiveness, but the experience of feeling forgiven is a gift of God's grace. On the other hand, we sometimes take forgiveness too lightly. It takes spiritual insight to have the gratitude and maturity to recognize God's gift of forgiveness.

By forgiving the man's sins, Jesus refuses to patronize him. Even though he is paralyzed and cannot move, he is still a sinner. To Jesus, he is more than an object of pity. He is a sinner like everyone else; he shares in common humanity. By forgiving his sins, Jesus acknowledges his responsibility for his actions. People with handicapping conditions do not want others to feel sorry for them. Jesus treats him with a kind of respect when he forgives his sins, and includes him in those who ought to repent because of the nearness of the dominion of God.

The church should be on the forefront of providing for the accessibility needs and employment for those with handicapping conditions. Accessibility means inclusion, and work means dignity. Any kind of advocacy, medical research, or empowerment for employment is an act of the church to release people from the constraints of their handicapping conditions.

I have talked to many Christians who were self-conscious about not being able to kneel at the communion rail, or even to come forward to take communion. One woman even told me that a former pastor did not serve her when she didn't kneel! The church makes every effort to put people at ease about the accessibility of the Lord's Supper. In one of my early churches, a woman with MS slowly made her way to the altar on communion Sundays. She knew we would serve her in her pew, but she wanted to take communion like everyone else. All of God's children should have that chance.

Preaching Strategies

Much of the substance of the passage revolves around the relationship between our physical bodies and our spiritual selves. I would not argue for a sharp break between these two spheres. As is well established, the New Testament authors did not understand a dichotomy between body and soul. The physical and spiritual are deeply intertwined. Nevertheless, we see a difference between them.

Abundant evidence exists that we in contemporary society place much emphasis on our physical bodies. Diet books, fad diets, and weight-loss clinics abound. Magazines for both men and women extol exercise programs that promise "sculpted abs," along with other attractive body parts. (Note: why do we need so many such articles? Any basic exercise program will do.) Plastic surgery for all kinds of deficiencies is popular. We are fascinated with models and movie stars with stunning good looks.

Certainly, our bodies are important. If our bodies don't work, that condition can limit our freedom, our ability to work, even our opportunities to love and be loved. A physical problem can bring down our spirits. Damage to parts of our brain can alter our personalities. Our bodies matter.

The passage points us away from our concern for our bodies to an emphasis on our spiritual health. The first words out of Jesus' mouth are "Son, your sins are forgiven." Before Jesus heals the man, he wipes his spiritual slate clean, restores the man's relationship with God and frees him from the power of sin. Forgiveness took priority. The importance of the spiritual aspect of the man's interaction with Jesus is underscored by the protest of the scribes. We do not know if the scribes would have protested if Jesus had healed only the man's body. For them, forgiveness was the more serious matter. As important as our bodies are, when we talk about forgiveness, we are dealing with holy matters. Only God can forgive sins. Only God can break the power of sin over our lives. The good news of the coming near of the dominion of God is that we are offered physical and spiritual wholeness.

Miracle Five

Breaking The Law To Fulfill It

The Text

One sabbath he was going through the grainfields; and as they made their way his disciples began to pluck heads of grain. The Pharisees said to him, "Look, why are they doing what is not lawful on the sabbath?" And he said to them, "Have you never read what David did when he and his companions were hungry and in need of food? He entered the house of God, when Abiathar was high priest, and ate the bread of the Presence, which is not lawful for any but the priests to eat, and he gave some to his companions." Then he said to them, "The sabbath was made for humankind, and not humankind for the sabbath; so the Son of Man is lord even of the sabbath."

Again he entered the synagogue, and a man was there who had a withered hand. They watched him to see whether he would cure him on the sabbath, so that they might accuse him. And he said to the man who had the withered hand, "Come forward." Then he said to them, "Is it lawful to do good or to do harm on the sabbath, to save life or to kill?" But they were silent. He looked around at them with anger; he was grieved at their hardness of heart and said to the man, "Stretch out your hand." He stretched it out, and his hand was restored. The Pharisees went out and immediately conspired with the Herodians against him, how to destroy him.

The conflict that began with the healing of the paralytic in Capernaum heats up in the rest of chapter 2. Jesus calls a tax collector (!) as a disciple, a decision that the Judean officials would consider suspicious (2:13-14). Two more incidents provoke the officials' ire. Jesus is seen eating with tax collectors and sinners, and his disciples do not fast (2:15-20). What kind of religious leader is Jesus anyway? Jesus proclaims that he has come to bring new wine, which needs new wine skins (2:22). Jesus' opponents presumably want to know what was wrong with the old wine. The conflict that was heating up throughout chapter 2 reaches full boil by the end of this pericope.

The lectionary committee has joined two stories for one Sunday. The two stories continue the conflict motif, and both deal with sabbath observance. Only the second story, the healing of the man's withered hand, is a miracle story.

Background

Despite concerted efforts by researchers over the course of at least two centuries, not much is known about the historical Pharisees. The Jewish historian, Josephus, tells us that the three main groups of Judaism in the first century were the Pharisees, the Sadducees, and the Essenes. We do not know much about how they functioned as a group. We are not certain whether they should be called a sect, a school, or some other designation. We do not know their socio-economic class or how they were organized. However they existed as a group, their main concern was ritual purity. They wanted to maintain Judean national identity under Roman rule. Without political power, they were reduced to maintaining their identity by obedience to food laws, ritual purity, and an emphasis on sabbath keeping and observance of religious festivals. They likely saw their efforts as an attempt to avoid assimilation into the Greco-Roman culture. They wanted to maintain the distinctiveness of Israelite identity in a society that either dismissed their claims, or was hostile to them. All we know of their interaction with Jesus is what we read in the New Testament. In the gospels, the Pharisees and Jesus are almost always in conflict, although in Luke some Pharisees warn Jesus to stay away from Herod (Luke

13:31). We know from the book of Acts that some Pharisees joined the early church (see, for example, Acts 15:5). The lack of historical information about the Pharisees is unfortunate. The New Testament writers portray them as caricatures. Because the gospel writers wanted to portray the Jesus movement as the true Israel, they put "spin" on the Pharisees' weaknesses. We can safely assume that the Pharisees were not monolithic. They likely were earnest and genuine in their attempts to be faithful to God in a hostile environment.

The commandment about sabbath observance is the one commandment among the Ten Commandments that is expressed very differently between the two versions. In the Exodus rendering of the Commandments, the rationale for the sabbath was that God had created the world in six days and rested on the sabbath. Observing the sabbath is a reminder of creation itself. In the Deuteronomy rendering, the rationale for sabbath observance is the exodus event. This rationale is, of course, narrower, but it encourages the people to remember the formation of their community and their special identity. In both versions, the sabbath rest extends to the whole household, even to animals. Even servants and slaves are to rest on the sabbath, making this commandment a kind of equalizer among family and social groups.

Sabbath observance is mentioned outside the Ten Commandments. Exodus 23:12 instructs sabbath observance and includes resident aliens. The purpose of sabbath observance here is relief and refreshment, a reminder that the sabbath instruction is a gift to humanity and to the animal world. Exodus 31:12-17 is more punitive. This passage does interpret the sabbath as a "sign between me and you throughout your generations" (v. 13) and speaks of the sense of remembrance and reflection as a rationale for sabbath observance. Moreover, it prescribes the death penalty for those who do work on the sabbath. Isaiah 58:13-14 offers spectacular promises to those who "refrain from trampling the sabbath." Those who consider the sabbath a "delight" will "take delight" in the Lord. Those who honor the sabbath will "ride upon the heights of the earth." This passage once again interprets the sabbath as a gift (see also Jeremiah 17:19-27).

59

The incident to which Jesus refers in the first of the stories occurs in 1 Samuel 21:1-6. David is on the run from Saul and goes to Nob. David asks the priest, Ahimelech, for five loaves of bread. Ahimelech says that he will give the bread to David as long as his men have kept themselves from women. David assures him that such is the case and takes the bread. The account in Mark contains some inaccuracies. The priest's name in 1 Samuel is Ahimelech, not Abiathar. Ahimelech was Abiathar's father. The text in 1 Samuel does not say, but only implies, that David gave some of the bread to his men.

Literary Analysis

In the first of the two stories in this pericope, the physical setting is difficult to visualize. The way the narrator describes the scene almost makes it sound as if Jesus is over to the side talking to the Pharisees while the disciples are walking through the grain field. However Mark wants us to understand the scene, the Pharisees' sudden appearance and question seem abrupt. The focus of the passage is on the conversation between Jesus and the Pharisees. We do not know the level of hostility in the voices of the Pharisees when they ask the question. We infer that they are troubled, but we do not know exactly how angry they are when they ask the question.

Jesus answers them by citing a narrative from 1 Samuel 21 about David eating the holy bread that only priests are allowed to eat. In the story from 1 Samuel, the priest, Ahimelech, seems to think that as long as the men have not recently had sex, it is permissible for them to eat the bread. Jesus' point in citing the story seems to be that in times of need, one can be flexible with strict rules. Jesus implies that the disciples are more than casually hungry. He describes David as "hungry and in need of food" (v. 25). Does this suggest that the disciples have already begun to make sacrifices in following Jesus? Is Jesus' point that the hunger and need of the disciples is so great, or that the Pharisees are too strict in their interpretation of the law on sabbath observance?

Jesus' second rationale for the behavior of the disciples is two pronouncements about the meaning of the sabbath, and his identity as "lord" of the sabbath. The first pronouncement is a statement in the form of a chiasm, "The sabbath was made for humankind and not humankind for the sabbath" (v. 27). Jesus' pronouncement picks up on the strands of Old Testament theology that interpret the sabbath as a gift (see above). The second pronouncement identifies Jesus as the Son of Man and as "lord of the sabbath." Curiously, the narrator does not tell us how the Pharisees react to Jesus' explanations of the behavior of the disciples. This lacuna puts the focus on Jesus' sayings. Perhaps the passage wants the reader to think that the power of Jesus' sayings is so strong that no rebuttal is possible.

In the second of the two stories, we are in no doubt about the attitude of the Pharisees. They are suspicious of Jesus. Instead of observing the sabbath, they are "observing" Jesus, waiting for him to give them ammunition. The Pharisees are the ones in the story who are on a quest. They want to find reason to accuse Jesus. As the story unfolds, they are successful in their quest.

This passage gives us a rare insight into Jesus' feelings. Jesus is angry at the Pharisees' hardness of heart. Jesus is passionate about his healing ministry, and cares deeply about people who suffer.

The narrator presents the man with the withered hand as the center of attention. The Pharisees notice him, and Jesus somehow knows that they have singled out this man with the withered hand. Jesus brings the man forward and asks the Pharisees a rhetorical question, "Is it lawful to do good or to do harm on the sabbath, to save life or to kill?" (v. 4). The silence of the Pharisees may mean that they have already made up their minds to oppose Jesus. In any case, they cannot respond to Jesus with authority as he did to them in the previous story. Jesus heals the man, but the healing has no positive effect on the Pharisees. The healing does not change their opinion, but may even stiffen their opposition. The conflict between Jesus and the Pharisees now has deadly implications. The ending of the story suggests that no chance for reconciliation exists. The conflict must play itself out.

Theological Reflection

These two texts raise the question of how we make ethical decisions. Obviously, the Pharisees and Jesus differ about what kinds of behavior represent a faithful response to God's grace and call. As stated above, we do not have access to what the historical Pharisees taught about adherence to the law (teachings) of the Old Testament. So, we have to contrast the position of the Pharisees as Mark presents it with the position of Jesus as Mark presents it. This is no easy task. We must discern these positions from the meager evidence of these two stories. The question of how we form ethical choices is a bigger issue than the sabbath observance question that dominates this text.

In the first story, the Pharisees claim that the behavior of the disciples (plucking heads of grain on the sabbath) is not *lawful*. Without trying to oversimplify their position, one can say that they seem to advocate in this instance an adherence to a particular interpretation of written law. Certain behaviors are permitted, and others are clearly not permitted. We do not know for sure if they would permit exceptions in cases of life or death, but to give them the benefit of the doubt, let's assume they would. This position seems rigid, but at least the options are clear. One can choose to obey or not to obey. As long as the behaviors are clearly defined, no ambiguity exists.

Jesus' position is more difficult to describe. His two rationales for the behavior of the disciples seem almost to conflict. His first rationale is that the Old Testament contains examples of people, including David, treating rules with some flexibility. Rules can be bent or broken in cases of human need, such as extreme hunger. Even in the 1 Samuel story, the priest required that the men refrain from sex before they ate the bread. The story does not advocate a moral free-for-all. Jesus' first pronouncement about the sabbath being made for humankind is consistent with this rationale. The sabbath is a gift. Jesus' second rationale is that because of his identity as Son of Man, he has more authority than the sabbath laws. He is "lord of the sabbath." The true way to find identity as the people of God is through him, not through the sabbath laws.

In the second story, Jesus more clearly advocates meeting people's needs as a correct ethical choice. Jesus does not say to meet people's need in contrast to observing the sabbath, but that meeting people's needs is a fulfillment of the sabbath requirement. Jesus overstates the case, because he will not be saving the man's life, and the Pharisees do not advocate that anyone should kill him. Nevertheless, Jesus proclaims that healing, making whole, is just the thing to do on a sabbath.

That leaves us with the question of how we know what we should and should not do. We might all affirm the principle of placing human need over rigid adherence to law. The question then becomes how we determine human need. How deep does the level of need have to be? What about when the needs of two or more people conflict? We appreciate the freedom from rigid adherence to the law, but the freedom Jesus gives us to make decisions can be dangerous. We are too subjective, too willing to justify our actions in most cases. The freedom Jesus gives us to make ethical decisions must be handled with care and spiritual maturity. Certainly, the Gospel of Mark, which calls the reader to take up the cross, does not give us license to do what we want. Nor, in the end, does Mark make human need the ultimate good. Certainly, Mark 9:43-48 suggests that bodily wholeness is not the ultimate good. For Mark, repentance because of the nearness of the dominion of God is the ultimate good.

Jesus plays a kingly role in this passage. He refers to himself as "lord (*kurios*) of the sabbath." He takes authority to interpret the law. He even compares himself to David (admittedly at a time before David was king). Jesus does not act as a king who abuses authority, but as one who acts to free his subjects from their bondage. He enables the disciples to assuage their hunger, and heals the man with the withered hand, so that he can work and take his place among the community of God's people.

Pastoral Reading

Our tendency as Christians is always to look down our noses at the Pharisees. We see them as the bad guys who keep messing with Jesus. They are the ones who just didn't get it. Before we become self-righteous, however, we should ask ourselves how much better we think we would do. Many Christians I know become just as furious as the Pharisees were, over certain matters. I pastor in Texas, a state where prayers can no longer be offered up before football games. In a recent Supreme Court case, many Christians were incensed at the possibility that the words "under God" might have been removed from the version of the Pledge of Allegiance recited in public schools. Many of the people in my churches over the last few years have been quite upset about both issues. Some denominations would be outraged if the youth proposed to hold a dance in the church's fellowship hall. If we can help our congregations understand that the Pharisees felt a similar anger, maybe we can get them to see Jesus' opponents with more ambiguity. They were more than just the crusty old religious leaders who refused to recognize who Jesus was when it was plain as day that he was the Messiah.

To the Pharisees, Jesus and his disciples treated the sabbath with disrespect. We don't know how hungry the disciples were in the first story. If it had been days since they ate, that's one thing. If breakfast was just wearing off, that's another. Exactly how hungry do you have to be before human need becomes more important than the sabbath restrictions? We all think that there are boundaries beyond which Christians just shouldn't go. Those boundaries are different for different people, but we all have them.

Even if the Pharisees could be persuaded that the man in the second story genuinely needed to be healed, they might have made the slippery slope argument. It starts with one healing on a sabbath, but where does it end? Once we start down the path of loosening our interpretations of moral directives, we raise the issue of where to stop. The slippery slope argument is not always persuasive or decisive, but it always is there to be reckoned with.

Most of us would agree that people of faith should not lie. Exodus 1 contains the story of Shiphrah and Puah, two Hebrew midwives. When the king of Egypt orders them to kill Hebrew boy babies to prevent the overpopulation of Hebrews, the two women lie to the Egyptian king. They claim that the Hebrew women give birth before they arrive, and so they have no opportunity to kill the

Hebrew boy babies. Most of us would agree that lying to save the life of a baby was justified, but can we not justify nearly every lie we tell?

These issues are not easy to resolve, which is why Christian ethicists still have jobs. We are in a rather uncertain area, where honest Christians disagree about right and wrong, not only on the big issues, but also on smaller, everyday matters. What this passage contributes to our ethical discussions is that human need plays an important part in our decisions. Neither human need nor bodily wholeness is the ultimate good, but pursuit of them is one of the ways in which we live out the new situation effected by the coming near of the dominion of God.

Modern Christians have misunderstood Jesus' attitude toward the sabbath. We are grateful to be free from rigid, strict enforcement of "blue laws" that kept stores and theaters closed on Sunday. Yet we have not replaced this rigid structure with a real understanding of sabbath as a time of rest, a time when we reflect on our relationship to God and remember who we are. The sabbath is not just a time to refrain from certain actions; it is a time to renew, restore, and heal. We have not recovered the understanding from the Old Testament and from this passage that the sabbath is a gift.

Preaching Strategies

This passage provides an excellent opportunity for preachers to help their congregations interpret the place of the law in Christian faith. Many Christians lack a spiritually healthy understanding of the law. The two extremes of misunderstanding are antinomianism on the one side and legalism on the other. Antinomianism often takes the form of believing that we are so free from the law that it has no value for us. Legalism wants to prescribe exactly what Christians should and should not do. Concerning the sabbath laws, antinomianism is the impulse not to treat Sunday (the Christian substitute for the Saturday sabbath) as any different from any other day. Legalism can take the form of "blue laws" that codify exactly what can and cannot be sold, or done, on Sunday.

The preacher's task is to enable the congregation to see the law as instruction or teaching (the Hebrew term "torah" can mean all three). Some passages from the Psalms may be helpful here. Psalm 19 extols the law as "reviving the soul," and "rejoicing the heart." Psalm 119 considers the Lord's ordinances to be a motivation to praise (v. 7) and the decrees to be a delight (v. 14). This sense of rejoicing in the law is foreign to most of us in the church. One goal of preaching from this passage could be to enable the congregation to recapture this sense of delight and praise for the law. The law is life giving, just as eating and healing are. When Jesus' disciples eat the grain and when Jesus heals the man's hand, life is affirmed.

The passage invites the preacher to focus specifically on the sabbath commandment. The preacher can instruct on how the sabbath commandment is a gift, how it is life giving and a delight. By careful observance of our time, and by setting aside time for remembering our relationship to God, we grow spiritually, a gift from God.

Miracle Six

The (Demonic) Empire Strikes Back

The Text

On that day, when evening had come, he said to them, "Let us go across to the other side." And leaving the crowd behind, they took him with them in the boat, just as he was. Other boats were with him. A great windstorm arose, and the waves beat into the boat, so that the boat was already being swamped. But he was in the stern, asleep on the cushion; and they woke him up and said to him, "Teacher, do you not care that we are perishing?" He woke up and rebuked the wind, and said to the sea, "Peace! Be still!" Then the wind ceased, and there was a dead calm. He said to them, "Why are you afraid? Have you still no faith?" And they were filled with great awe and said to one another, "Who then is this, that even the wind and the sea obey him?"

Throughout chapter 4 Jesus has been teaching the crowds in parables. The general theme of the parables has been the inevitability of the kingdom of God. Jesus has been sitting in a boat while the crowd gathered at the sea. When Jesus leaves the crowd to go across the sea, a storm whips up — perhaps a threat to the inevitability of the kingdom! Jesus is going to Gentile territory to expand his mission. To this point the demons have been altogether helpless against the ministry of Jesus. Now they seem to stage a frontal attack.

67

Background

Throughout much of the Old Testament the sea is more than just water. At the least the sea represents danger; at the most it is the home of chaotic and even demonic forces. In creation narratives, poetry, and vision reports, the Old Testament writers paint a dark, mysterious, and treacherous portrait of the sea.

As chapter 1 of Genesis opens, the dark, murky waters of chaos are raging and out of control. God's first act of creation is to bring calm and order to the tempestuous waters of chaos. God's life-giving breath (*ruah*) blows over the shapeless waters to create room for life. Although the water is unruly, God controls the water to enact God's purposes.

Isaiah 27:1 portrays the sea as the home of a fearsome, rebellious beast. "On that day, the Lord with his cruel and great and strong sword will punish Leviathan the fleeing serpent, Leviathan the twisting serpent, and he will kill the dragon that is in the sea." Leviathan is a mythological beast, which appears in creation stories from the ancient near east that may have influenced the creation narratives and poems in the Old Testament. Leviathan in Isaiah is more than a sort of Hebrew Loch Ness monster. God's battle with Leviathan is a cosmic battle to rid the world of evil. Leviathan is mentioned in Psalm 74:13-14 and Job 41.

Daniel 7 is an apocalyptic text, written at a time of deep crisis for the Jewish community. Jerusalem was under severe persecution from the Syrian ruler, Antiochus IV. In chapter 7, Daniel has a dream in which four beasts arise from the sea. These beasts are ghastly in appearance, and the fourth is the most terrible of all. These beasts represent the four kingdoms of Babylon, Media, Persia, and Greece. The beasts are the otherworldly counterparts to the four earthly kingdoms. Daniel 7 is proclaiming through the vision that the conflict on earth is part of a cosmic evil that only God can fight. The beasts arise from the sea, the home of evil beings.

Some texts represent the sea as dangerous, but not necessarily demonic. In the book of Jonah, the title character tries to flee from the presence of the Lord (an impossible task!) by sailing to Tarshish. The Lord has called him to go to Nineveh. While he is on the boat,

68

a storm erupts which threatens to sink the boat. The cause of the storm is that God "hurled a great wind upon the sea" (Jonah 1:4). Despite the best efforts of the sailors, they cannot row against the storm. They are forced to throw Jonah overboard, at which point the sea grows calm. In this story, the sea is completely under the Lord's control. The sea performs God's will by preventing Jonah's flight.

Psalm 107 is a pilgrimage psalm celebrating the providence of the Lord in bringing the pilgrims safely to Jerusalem. Starting in verse 23, the psalm recounts the peril of sailors who encounter a storm on the sea. Without offering an explanation, the psalmist attributes the storm to the Lord's actions. "For he commanded and raised the stormy wind, which lifted up the waves of the sea" (v. 25). The sailors, physically unable to cope with the storm, grow frightened. The storm abates when they cry out to the Lord. After quieting the storm, the Lord brings them to their destination. The psalmist does not attribute the storm to the sinfulness of the sailors or the desire of the Lord to test their faith. Even though the Lord created the storm, the psalmist considers the Lord's protection and guidance in the storm to be an example of the Lord's "steadfast love" (v. 31).

Psalm 3 contains a verse that suggests peaceful sleep is a sign of one's trust in the Lord. "I lie down and sleep; I wake again, for the Lord sustains me" (v. 5). Psalm 4:8 has a similar sentiment, "I will both lie down and sleep in peace; for you alone, O Lord, make me lie down in safety." Perhaps Jesus' sleep in the boat in verse 38 indicates his trust in God.

Literary Analysis

This story is driven mostly by the action. The dialogue is sparse, even if it is important. The drama is conveyed through the skill of the narrator, who strikes a good balance between subtlety and powerful description.

The narrator sets the stage in verse 1. The day is drawing to a close. Jesus has spent the day preaching from a boat. The darkness of night creates a sinister mood (see Mark 15:33 for an example of darkness as an image of evil). Jesus directs the disciples to cross the sea to the other side. The fact that other boats are with them means that the demonic forces can wipe out not only Jesus, but also the whole movement in one fell swoop. The storm arises suddenly and unexpectedly. Wouldn't experienced fishermen have noticed signs of a potential storm? The narrator vividly describes the terror and power of the storm, "the waves beat into the boat, so that the boat was already being swamped" (v. 37).

In sharp contrast to the raging storm, Jesus sleeps peacefully in the stern. Whatever the historicity of this story, surely this detail is a literary technique. Who could sleep through such a storm? The disciples interpret Jesus' sleep as a lack of concern for their safety. They ask frantically, "Teacher, do you not care that we are perishing?" (v. 38) Jesus' sleep seems to convey a sense of trust, a sense that Jesus does not feel threatened by the storm.

The narrator never says explicitly that the storm is the work of demons. The Old Testament background and the anxiety and hostility of the demons in the first four chapters of the book suggest that the storm has a deeper meaning. The biggest clue is that when Jesus wakes up, he "rebukes" the wind, and speaks to the sea, as though the sea were an entity. One translator even renders Jesus' words to the storm as "Silence! Shut up!"[1] (The Anchor Bible, v. 39, compare the NRSV "Peace! Be still!") All of these clues add up to the conclusion that the storm is a demon or demonic force attempting to destroy Jesus. In a reversal of the Genesis 1 creation narrative, the sea seeks to revert to chaos. Now, both human forces (3:6) and demonic forces are trying to destroy Jesus, and maybe the disciples, as well.

Jesus' words to the disciples express a sense of exasperation. After all of the healings and exorcisms, they still did not have faith. To their credit, they did wake Jesus up, apparently under the assumption that he could calm the storm. One wonders what Jesus expected the disciples to do. Should they have simply continued in the face of the storm? Should they have tried to rebuke the storm themselves? Should they have spoken to Jesus with more calm and assurance, "Jesus, not that we're worried, but when you get a minute, could you calm down this storm?"

The text compares two types of fear. Jesus asks the disciples why they are afraid (v. 40). This fear is an act of unfaith, a lack of trust in Jesus' power. The narrator tells us that at the end of the incident, the disciples are filled with great awe. This is proper awe in the presence of the holy.

The disciples' rhetorical question at the end of the passage, "Who is this, that even the wind and the sea obey him?" is the question Mark wants to leave the reader asking. It sums up the story. The reader is forced to answer the question. Given what we know about the sea, who could possibly control it? The only answer is that the Son of God could, but the disciples are still not ready to give that answer.

Theological Reflection

The passage raises questions about how we understand our relationship to nature. Nature is part of God's creation. On the one hand, nature is a source of endless delight: forests, meadows, ponds, the beach, and adorable furry creatures. On the other hand, nature is dangerous and forbidding: hurricanes, tornadoes, floods, droughts, and ferocious predators. People stand in an ambiguous relationship with nature. It is both friend and foe. We cannot separate ourselves from nature. We live in the midst of nature and must make our way within it.

We moderns are not comfortable saying that a storm is caused by demons. Tornadoes, hurricanes, floods, and other storms do seem almost cruel. We all understand when someone says a dark, cloudy sky looks "angry." Tornadoes seem almost vindictive in the damage they do. When we move beyond weather phenomena and look at the animal kingdom, we still see everything from nuisance to the fight for survival to downright cruelty (watch a cat with a rodent). My wife often asks me what God was thinking when flies, mosquitoes, and spiders were created. Beyond the nuisance factor of bugs, we see much disharmony in the animal kingdom. Carnivores exist by hunting and eating other creatures. Watch a nature documentary and notice the terror in the eyes of a rabbit about to be caught by predator. Sharks and snakes even have a malevolent visage.

This passage, as were the physical healings, is a manifestation of the coming near of the dominion of God. Mark might attribute the deadliness of nature to demons; we might not agree. Nevertheless, part of the coming near of the dominion of God is reconciliation between people and nature and the parts of nature. When the realm of God comes in its fullness, all of creation will be healed, including nature. The prophet Isaiah paints a beautiful picture of the reconciliation and redemption of nature. "The wolf shall live with the lamb, the leopard shall lie down with the kid, the calf and the lion and the fatling together, and a little child shall lead them. The cow and the bear shall graze, their young shall lie down together; and the lion shall eat straw like the ox. The nursing child shall play over the hole of the asp, and the weaned child shall put its hand on the adder's den" (Isaiah 11:6-8).

Scholars are agreed that the storm in this passage has layers of meaning. The storm represents the untamed forces of nature, as well as the efforts of demonic forces to wipe out Jesus and his followers. On another level, the storm represents persecution. The Gospel of Mark was likely written at a time when the church was undergoing persecution under Nero and the Roman society in general. In most areas of the Mediterranean world now separated from the synagogue and becoming an increasingly Gentile movement, the church was gradually losing the protection Rome had granted that ancient community. The boat was an early symbol of the church. Part of the message of this passage to the early church was to hang in there; the church will survive the storms of persecution. The "other boats" did not have Jesus in them, but (presumably) they survived the storm, too. The church no longer has Jesus present with it, but will survive the storms of the surrounding culture, which were likely to be hostile and even demonic. The church should have the faith Jesus expects of the disciples, even in rough waters.

Pastoral Reading

This passage raises once again the question of what it means to have faith. When the four men brought their paralyzed companion to Jesus, part of their faith was persistence (Mark 2:1-12). They took creative, bold, even pushy action. In this story, faith has to do with not being afraid in a storm. Jesus scolded the disciples for showing fear, which Jesus interpreted as a lack of faith (v. 40). We may wonder how we best can live out this kind of faith. At its most literal it would mean courage in a storm. Does faith mean that if you live in a coastal area, and a hurricane is coming your way, you stay put and don't evacuate? Beyond this whimsical example, where does courageous faith end and reckless disregard for danger begin?

The place where we need courageous faith the most is in the church's ministry. Often, a church (or larger body) has to step out into a ministry that is uncertain. A building campaign, a new outreach, or a change of location can bring risks. One area of ministry that always demands courage is standing up against injustice. As Old Testament prophets such as Micah and Amos and modern-day prophets such as Martin Luther King, Jr., and Oscar Romero found out, taking a stand for justice involves risk. Faith does not guarantee that our ministry for justice will be "successful" as the world defines success. We will not be protected from the storms of anger, resistance, or even an assassin's bullet. Nevertheless, faith carries us through in these justice ministries, trusting God for the real success of the ministry.

The church, of course, is very active in ministries with people who have been affected by storms: tornadoes, hurricanes, floods, and the like. Churches help with emergency care, rebuilding homes, economic recovery, and a host of other ministries.

We can learn something from Jesus' sleep on the boat. The disciples interpret Jesus' sleep as a lack of concern. Sometimes, we face situations in which we can do nothing. We have taken our best shot, or circumstances prevent our intervention. In those cases, we can trust that God is active in ways we cannot see. H. Richard Niebuhr wrote an essay in the '30s titled, "The Grace of Doing Nothing." He was writing to defend a pacifist stance in the war between Japan and China. Whether one is a pacifist or not, some of what Niebuhr says is instructive. He contrasts the Christian way of doing nothing with pessimism, cynicism, and protecting the status quo. He declares that the Christian way of doing nothing "appears to be highly impracticable because it rests on the well-nigh obsolete faith that there is a real God."[2] Niebuhr counsels patience in situations where we can do nothing. He says, though, that it is "a patience that is full of hope, and is based on faith."[3] Jesus' sleep is not a lack of concern, but a trust in God. In situations where we feel helpless to act or change things, we can still trust in God, not naively, but in faith and hope.

Preaching Strategies

The different layers of meaning for the storm in this passage give the preacher many starting points for a sermon. Focusing on the storm as an act of nature could lead to a sermon on the way we experience nature as both friend and foe. We refresh ourselves in nature, but we also fear nature. Because nature is fearful, we long for God to redeem creation. The church has a ministry to those who are displaced, physically injured, or economically ruined by weather phenomena.

A focus on the storm as an allusion to persecution in the early church could lead to a sermon on the ways in which the church continues to experience persecution. In many countries the church is persecuted violently. Often the church encounters backlash in its struggle to pursue justice. The rich, powerful, and comfortable resist attempts to produce equitable division of economic resources, goods, and services. Martin Luther King, Jr., tells of his early days in the Montgomery bus boycott. Acknowledging that he had led a sheltered life until he began his pastorate in Alabama, King relates how stressful the resistance to justice was during the boycott. Because of his leadership in the boycott he began to receive threatening phone calls. One night, after a particularly hateful call, he could not go back to sleep. He entered into intense, nearly desperate prayer. In response to his prayer, he experienced a genuine sense of God's presence. Shortly after King's night of prayer, his home was bombed. Even with such danger, the feeling of God's presence persisted. King shares the epiphany: "My experience with God had given me a new strength and trust. I knew now that God is able to give us the interior resources to face the storms and problems of life."[4] King uses the metaphor of storms to describe the backlash against his quest for justice. His sense of peace reminds us of Jesus' faithful sleep in the boat.

One can interpret the storm in this passage as an outbreak of demonic hostility toward Jesus and his disciples. The demonic forces seek to destroy Jesus and his disciples. On this level, the demonic forces use God's creation against the Son of God. This level of meaning reminds the church that it is in a constant spiritual battle. The demonic forces use every tool to corrupt and thwart the work of the church, and to resist God's will for creation. Even the structures of the church itself can be used against the church. The church's weapons in this spiritual battle are prayer, worship, the sacraments, and faith.

---

1. Joel Marcus, *Mark 1-8: A New Translation with Introduction and Commentary* (The Anchor Bible), ed. William Foxwell Albright and David Noel Freedman, no. 27 (New York: Doubleday, 1999), p. 332.

2. *Christian Century*, 49 March 23, 1932, p. 379, article 378-380.

3. *Ibid.*, p. 380.

4. *Strength to Love* (Philadelphia: Fortress Press, 1963), p. 114.

Miracle Seven

The Gift Of Life
For The Givers Of Life

The Text

When Jesus had crossed again in the boat to the other side, a great crowd gathered around him; and he was by the sea. Then one of the leaders of the synagogue named Jairus came and, when he saw him, fell at his feet and begged him repeatedly, "My little daughter is at the point of death. Come and lay your hands on her, so that she may be made well, and live." So he went with him.

And a large crowd followed him and pressed in on him. Now there was a woman who had been suffering from hemorrhages for twelve years. She had endured much under many physicians, and had spent all that she had; and she was no better, but rather grew worse. She had heard about Jesus, and came up behind him in the crowd and touched his cloak, for she said, "If I but touch his clothes, I will be made well." Immediately her hemorrhage stopped; and she felt in her body that she was healed of her disease. Immediately aware that power had gone forth from him, Jesus turned about in the crowd and said, "Who touched my clothes?" And his disciples said to him, "You see the crowd pressing in on you; how can you say, 'Who touched me?'" He looked all around to see who had done it. But the woman, knowing what had happened to her, came in fear and trembling, fell down before him, and told him the whole truth. He said to her, "Daughter, your faith has made you well; go in peace, and be healed of your disease."

While he was still speaking, some people came from the leader's house to say, "Your daughter is dead. Why trouble the teacher any further?" But overhearing what they said, Jesus said to the leader of the synagogue, "Do not fear, only believe." He allowed no one to follow him except Peter, James, and John, the brother of James. When they came to the house of the leader of the synagogue, he saw a commotion, people weeping and wailing loudly. When he had entered, he said to them, "Why do you make a commotion and weep? The child is not dead but sleeping." And they laughed at him. Then he put them all outside, and took the child's father and mother and those who were with him, and went in where the child was. He took her by the hand and said to her, "Talitha cum," which means, "Little girl, get up!" And immediately the girl got up and began to walk about (she was twelve years of age). At this they were overcome with amazement. He strictly ordered that no one should know this, and told them to give her something to eat.

After Jesus calms the storm on the sea, he and the disciples land in Gentile territory. There Jesus encounters the Gerasene demoniac, who is possessed by a demon named "legion" (a jab at the Roman occupying army?). Jesus sends the demons into pigs, which then rush into the sea. After ridding the Gentiles of demons, Jesus crosses back into Israelite territory. Ironically, after Jesus purges the area of demons, the crowds want him to leave (5:17). Even though the demons are in the sea once again, they make no trouble as Jesus crosses over.

Once Jesus is back in Jewish territory, the crowds again surround him and he is confronted with human need. The two intertwined stories in this section are both the most interesting, and perhaps the most important of the stories this book will treat. The characters in these stories are the best developed and the narration is the most sophisticated of any of the Marcan miracle accounts. The stories may be the most important because they concern issues of life, death, and resurrection.

Background

Assuming that the woman with the hemorrhage faced the prospect of dying (since her condition had grown worse), these two stories take us to the brink of the ultimate questions about the purpose of life and the meaning of death. The Old Testament has much to teach about both questions.

The two creation narratives in the book of Genesis affirm that God is the author of life. God treasures the creation and values all life. The relationship between God and people is unique and God's charge to people to care for the rest of creation is an expression of that uniqueness. A consistent theme in the creation narratives is God's intention to produce and sustain life. God makes space for life and sets up the conditions for life to thrive. The first mention of death is Genesis 2:17 where the Lord God warns the newly created man not to eat of the tree of the knowledge of good and evil, saying, "for in the day that you eat of it you shall die." As everyone knows the man and the subsequently created woman eat from the tree, exposing themselves to the threat of death. The dialogue in Genesis 3:22-24 suggests that death was not originally part of God's intention for creation. Death is a consequence of disobedience. Death is in one sense a punishment but it is also a protection. Death is a check on the destructiveness of human sin.

Throughout most of the Old Testament, the writers do not affirm much of a life after death. It is not quite accurate to say that the Old Testament writers believe that after death people have only complete oblivion ahead of them. The dead go to the realm of Sheol, a murky, mysterious place that offers only a kind of shadowy existence. The psalmists who mention Sheol do not look forward to existence there. The poet of Psalm 6 expects that in Sheol he will not be able to praise or even remember the Lord anymore. "For in death there is no remembrance of you; in Sheol who can give you praise?" (Psalm 6:5, compare Paul in Philippians 1:23, where he looks forward to death because he will be with Christ). With no expectation of life after death, the writers of the Old Testament considered a short life to be especially tragic. Isaiah's description of the new heaven and new earth contains the promise that no one will have to suffer the death of a child. That is a promise both for parents and for children, who can lead a long life (Isaiah 65: 20). Jephthah's daughter mourned that she would die before she could marry and have children (Judges 11:37-40).

Belief in resurrection did not develop until late in Old Testament thought. Psalm 73:24 seems to suggest some expectation of some relationship with God after death, but the verse is not clear. Isaiah 26:19 is an ambiguous verse that likely refers to the reformation of the people of Judah after exile (cf. Ezekiel 37:1-14). Resurrection is explicitly affirmed in Daniel 12:2, "Many of those who sleep in the dust of the earth shall awake, some to everlasting life, and some to shame and everlasting contempt." The second-century B.C.E. Syrian tyrant, Antiochus IV, proscribed the religion of the Judeans. Judeans who continued to observe Torah regulations, such as circumcisions and food laws, were executed. This affirmation of resurrection in Daniel represents the conviction that Antiochus would not defeat God's purposes. God would have the last word. The question in Daniel 12:2 is how extensive the resurrection would be. In all likelihood, Daniel affirms only that those whom Antiochus had executed would be raised to everlasting life. Those who perpetrated the persecution, and those Judeans who cooperated with the persecutors, or who gave in to the pressure, would be raised to everlasting contempt. In the intertestamental period the belief in resurrection evolved. 2 Maccabees contains a narrative in which seven brothers and their mother endure torture at the hands of Antiochus. They encourage one another with the assurance of resurrection. At the time of Jesus, not all Judeans affirmed resurrection, however.

Besides belief in resurrection, the Old Testament contains stories about people who do not die (Enoch in Genesis 5:24 and Elijah in 2 Kings 2:11) or who are raised back to life. These stories demonstrate God's power over life and death and the life-giving power bequeathed to prophets. Two narratives about prophets raising children back to life give important background to the story of Jairus' daughter.

In 1 Kings 17, Elijah announces a drought as a sign that the Lord is more powerful than Baal, the Canaanite fertility god. During the famine, Elijah meets a Phoenician woman who is out of food and expects that she and her son will die soon. Elijah promises her that her food will last until the end of the drought. Subsequently, the woman's son dies of an illness. Elijah raises the boy to life by stretching himself out upon the boy's body. The woman initially thinks that the death of her son is the result of her sinfulness and that Elijah exposes that sinfulness (17:18). By the end of the story, after her son is raised, she interprets the miracle as evidence of the Lord's presence and power with Elijah (v. 24).

In 2 Kings 4, Elisha encounters a Shunamite woman who provided shelter and meals for him on his travels. In gratitude, Elisha promises her a son. A few years later, the boy dies of what could be heatstroke or an aneurysm. Elisha raises the boy back to life by lying on top of him. The boy's death had undone an earlier miracle (the birth itself), and another miracle was needed to bring him back (2 Kings 4:8-37). That both Elijah and Elisha could raise dead children indicates that the power was God's, not that of the prophet. Both stories proclaim God's grace in the face of the grief of the death of children.

The woman with the hemorrhage was, of course, ritually unclean. The laws about a woman being unclean during menstruation are found in Leviticus 15. A woman was unclean during her regular cycle (v. 19), and, if her bleeding continued after her regular cycle, as in the case of the woman in Mark. Anyone who touched her and everything she touched also were unclean. On a deeper level, the woman was estranged from her own body. In a sense, her reproductive system had turned against her. That God had blessed and worked through the female reproductive system is affirmed in the Old Testament. In the first creation story, God instructs the man and woman to "be fruitful and multiply" (Genesis 1:28). God opened the wombs of barren women such as Sarah (Genesis 21:1-2) and Hannah (1 Samuel 1:20). Eve was the "mother of all living" (Genesis 3:20). What was intended to be a blessing had, for the woman in our story, become a curse.

Literary Analysis
Each of these stories by itself is interesting. Intertwined as they are in a kind of story "sandwich" (intercalation), they are a

fascinating display of Mark's narrative skill and theological insight. The characters, the heightening of the tension, the connections between the two stories, and the rhetorical flourishes all draw us into a powerful narrative sequence.

The Characters

Jairus is a synagogue leader. He has duties concerned with making the worship services go smoothly and in an orderly way in the synagogue. As he abruptly appears in the story, he demonstrates spontaneous worship, falling at Jesus' feet. His concern for his daughter is touching and endearing. He places himself in a humble and subordinate posture for her sake. He may even risk the ire of the other Judean leaders, who are hostile to Jesus. Here is an Israelite leader who seeks Jesus out. Does recognition of need make one predisposed to seek out Jesus, and not to oppose him?

The woman elicits our sympathy. Through no fault of her own she is an outcast. She is a victim of legalism, and of incompetent or corrupt physicians. She is so lonely that she converses only with herself. She is a victim of the legal system, but still upholds it, hoping to acquire healing without contaminating Jesus (or at least in such a way that no one would know he was contaminated). When Jesus discovers what she has done, she is honest, even though she is frightened. In many ways, she is a contrast to Jairus. He is named in the story; she is not. He has a family; she has been isolated from hers. He is a synagogue leader; she cannot worship with the community. He can approach Jesus directly; she must act surreptitiously.

The crowds and the "extras" in the story play a significant role. The crowds once again demonstrate Jesus' popularity at this point in his ministry. They seem almost to restrict Jesus' movement (v. 24). They provide an opportunity for the woman to approach Jesus unnoticed and, consequently, are integral to the plot. After the woman is healed, she faces a choice. She can admit that she was the one who touched Jesus or she can fade back into the crowd. The people who come from Jairus' house and the mourners are not the same people as the crowd, but they are part of the generic characters in the story. The people who come from Jairus' house to report the death of the little girl add to the suspense and to the sense of wonder about her raising. Those who scoff and laugh at Jesus for saying the girl is only sleeping represent the presence of doubt and let us know that Jesus' raising the girl back to life went against expectations. Peter, James, and John are not just generic characters, but they do not speak or do much. Their presence signals that something important is about to happen. (See 9:2-8, where Peter, James, and John are present at the Transfiguration.)

Although Jesus shows his characteristic compassion and power, his actions in this narrative contradict what we know of him from elsewhere in Mark. The plot development suggests that the delay in Jesus getting to the bedside of the girl may have led to her death. Elsewhere in Mark, however, Jesus can cast out a demon without being present (7:24-30). Jesus knows the conversation of the scribes "in his spirit," but doesn't know who has touched the hem of his garments. Jesus orders everyone to keep the healing a secret, even though crowds already surround him, and many people saw what happened. (Here, Mark is probably making a theological point that people are not yet ready to understand the resurrection, because they have not seen the cross.) Despite these curiosities, Jesus is still the gracious healer. He leaves readily to go with Jairus, speaks tenderly to the woman, and acts gently with the little girl.

Literary techniques abound in these narratives. The insertion of the story of the woman adds suspense to the story of Jairus and his daughter. The description of the woman adds up phrases, which accentuate the seriousness of her plight ("suffering from hemorrhages," "endured much," "spent all she had," "was no better, but rather grew worse"). The message of the people from Jairus' house ("your daughter is dead"), along with the weeping and wailing, creates an initial disappointment that highlights the joy of the girl's raising (vv. 35-38). Many commentators have noted the use of sensory words in this passage. Jairus "saw" Jesus, the woman "heard" about Jesus, and "felt" her healing, Jesus was aware that power went out of him, Jesus "overhears" the words of the people from Jairus' house (the Greek word there may mean "ignored"). These terms help give an immediacy to the story so that we can imagine ourselves in the tale itself. Jesus, taking the girl by the hand, and her walking around, add to this effect.

Theological Reflection

Jesus raising the little girl to life is a manifestation of Jesus' power over life and death and is a foreshadowing of his own resurrection. Jesus' comment that the girl is not dead but asleep is strange within the context of the story, since sleep can be a euphemism for death. Mark's point seems to be that even death is not final. The biblical writers treat death as more than just the absence of life. Death is presented as a power or a force that is active and malevolent. The prophet Hosea writes of death and Sheol as active powers that God might use to punish the people for their sins. "Shall I ransom them from the power of Sheol? Shall I redeem them from Death? O Death, where are your plagues? O Sheol, where is your destruction?" (Hosea 13:14). Paul cites this verse, but changes the tone. Paul taunts Death and Sheol, not as God's agents for punishment, but as foes defeated by Christ's resurrection. "Death has been swallowed up in victory. Where, O death is your victory? Where, O death is your sting? The sting of death is sin, and the power of sin is the law. But thanks be to God, who gives us the victory through our Lord Jesus Christ" (1 Corinthians 15:54-57). Mark does not use this kind of language, but the scene in the passage is a battle between Jesus and the power of death. The reader is in suspense as to who will win. As with the demons and unclean spirits, Jesus' victory over death is effortless. He shows here who will win the conflict that is now brewing with the demonic forces and with the earthly leaders who are trying to destroy him. Theologically, we can affirm that God will win the ultimate battle with death.

By wrapping the story of the woman with the hemorrhage inside the story of Jairus' daughter, Mark makes an important theological point. The story of the raising of Jairus' daughter confirms Jesus' power over death itself. Presumably, Jairus' daughter would die again someday. Raising her to life now points toward God's eschatological victory over death. The healing of the woman with the hemorrhage points toward the life and wholeness available now. God offers us life and wholeness in the eschaton, but we do not have to wait to begin experiencing that life.

Within the Gospel of Mark, this story presents a great irony. Jesus has power over death and offers life, but calls his disciples to take up the cross and die (chapter 8). In reality, it is only because Jesus offers eschatological life that he can call his disciples to die. The death to which Jesus calls his disciples is not an ultimate death. It is a death that leads to life. That Jesus so clearly celebrates and offers life in this passage means that the call to take up the cross is not a morbid rejection of life or a call to suffering for the sake of suffering. The call to take up the cross is a call to confront the demonic and human forces that seek to thwart God's will for creation. Those forces may seem to have power, and do have the power to kill Jesus' followers, but those forces do not have ultimate power over life and death.

Pastoral Reading

As powerful and tender as this passage is, it might actually be depressing to some people. We take comfort in the promise of the resurrection, but those who have lost a child want the child back *now*. Losing a child is one of the most painful experiences a person can undergo. We in the church now can offer healing for grief, but often what the grieving parent wants is what Jairus got, the child restored. Nevertheless, this passage provides the church an opportunity to engage in grief ministry. Our words and actions in times of grief are so important. People often want to rush grieving people through the process. I sometimes think some people believe that a grieving person should have one good cry and then get over it. Grief is hard work and takes time. People grieve at their own pace, and not as their friends and families seem to want them to. It is true that some people obsess over the death of a loved one, and never learn to let go. The church must be there in those situations, too. Still, we must not mistake the normal process of grief for pathological grief.

John Claypool, an Episcopal priest, writes about his experience of losing a young daughter to leukemia. He describes the emotional agony of watching her suffer. In a particularly poignant section, he relates how he prayed by her bedside as she bit a rag to endure the pain. His daughter's illness and death caused Claypool to question the existence of God and the rationality of life. He explains his long struggle to deal with his grief and to find courage in the midst of his questions and hurt. As he reflects on the reminders of his daughter's life he concludes that of the alternatives available to him he must choose gratitude. "... I can dissolve in remorse that all of this is gone forever; or, focusing on the wonder that she was given to us at all, I can learn to be grateful that we shared life, even for an all-too-short ten years."[1]

The woman with the hemorrhage is estranged from her womanhood. Her problem originates in a physical symptom, a dysfunctional menstrual flow. Her femininity should be a source of joy, but it has become a burden. Part of Jesus' healing of her physical condition is the restoration of her ability to be herself as a woman. Even women who are physically healthy face conflicts and ambiguities concerning society's expectations about femininity. Women often find themselves in tension about their roles in society. For example, if toughness is not a quality they wish to cultivate, because they think it will make them less compassionate, they may be frustrated because of the expectation they will be tough in the workplace. Women face issues of sexual harassment and patronization that men may not encounter. A controversy has recently arisen at Duke University because a study suggested that undergraduate women there face pressure to achieve "effortless perfection."[2] They are expected to be intelligent, athletic, witty, attractive, and popular without exerting discernable effort. Perhaps the woman in this passage can give us resources to talk about how women can reconcile their roles in society with their understanding of femininity.

In three of the cases in which Jesus has healed women, the woman healed has faced the threat of death. Simon's mother-in-law may have had malaria, a potentially deadly disease. The woman with the hemorrhage was getting worse; her body might not have survived further loss of blood. Jairus' daughter had already died. By staking so much on the healing of women, Mark seems to be honoring women's roles as life-givers and nurturers. He seems especially to do that in this passage in chapter 5. Jairus' daughter is just at the age of transition between girl and woman. She will soon be at childbearing age. The woman has a condition that prevents her from bearing children. Both women are given back their capacity to be life-givers.

When Jesus greets the woman he has just healed as "daughter," he restores her to relationship (5:34). She has been isolated from her family, but Jesus greets her as a family member. The church often serves as a surrogate family for some people. Whether it is college students far from home, those whose family life is destructive, or people who simply don't have much family, the church can be a place for people to experience the intimacy and support a family should provide.

Preaching Strategies

The narrative artistry of this passage is an incentive for the preacher to employ narrative strategies for the sermon. To be sure, the passage brims with rich theology. It treats matters of life, death, grief, womanhood, resurrection, suffering, and faith. Yet the preacher can strive, as Mark does, to communicate this theological feast through a narrative structure. The passage gives ample resources for narrative preaching. Jairus and the woman are both sympathetic characters, described by Mark with sufficient depth to enable the preacher to present them to the congregation engagingly. The narrative contains suspense, drama, and a range of emotions.

One significant challenge of preaching this passage is weaving the two stories together in one sermon. Although preaching only one story is easier, Mark has connected the stories so carefully that separating them would be a disservice both to the pericope and to the congregation. The preacher can skillfully maintain suspense while moving from the first part of the passage about Jairus' daughter to the story of the woman and back again. Mark links the stories by the crowd following Jesus from one scene to the next (5:24) and by Jesus receiving the news of the girl's death while still speaking to the woman (5:35). The preacher can be careful to link the parts of the sermon in a continuous narrative.

Skillful narration will enable the congregation to experience the power of healing and new life through the characters themselves. Jairus personifies the anxiety of a parent of a sick child. We might assume that in verse 36 he is caught between faith and doubt. The people at Jairus' house personify grief and cynicism (their laughter in verse 40). The woman personifies the desperation of one who has nowhere else to turn and nothing left to lose. They both personify the joy of healing, restoration, and reconciliation. The more skillfully we can present them to our congregations the more fully they can experience God's grace in their own situations.

1. "Life is a Gift," in *A Chorus of Witnesses: Model Sermons for Today's Preacher*, ed. By Thomas G. Long and Cornelius Planting, Jr. (Grand Rapids: William B. Eerdmanns Publishing Company, 1994), pp. 129-130.

2. Kiya Bajpai, "Talking About 'Effortless Perfection,' " *Duke Chronicle* April 16, 2004, <www.chronicle.duke.edu>.

Miracle Eight

Getting Back Into The Conversation

The Text

Then he returned from the region of Tyre, and went by way of Sidon towards the Sea of Galilee, in the region of the Decapolis. They brought to him a deaf man who had an impediment in his speech; and they begged him to lay his hand on him. He took him aside in private, away from the crowd, and put his fingers into his ears, and he spat and touched his tongue. Then looking up to heaven, he sighed and said to him, "Ephphatha," that is, "Be opened." And immediately his ears were opened, his tongue was released, and he spoke plainly. Then Jesus ordered them to tell no one; but the more he ordered them, the more zealously they proclaimed it. They were astounded beyond measure, saying, "He has done everything well; he even makes the deaf to hear and the mute to speak."

This little story is often neglected, dwarfed by the more well-known stories of the miraculous feeding and the Syrophoenician woman and her daughter that come before it. Matthew and Luke do not include a parallel to it in their gospels. Chapter 8 is a turning point in the Gospel of Mark: Jesus begins talking about his death. It is easy to lose this story in the shuffle. As we will see, though, the story makes crucial theological points in Mark.

Background

The Old Testament does not contain stories about the deaf being healed, which makes this account in Mark unique in the Bible. Nevertheless, the Old Testament has much to say about the importance of the sense of hearing and of speaking. Hearing and speaking affect relationships among people and between people and God, and have implications for the creation itself.

The world of the Old Testament was largely an oral culture. Literacy rates were low, and people communicated primarily by speaking and hearing. I do not have information about any sort of sign language, but any such system likely would have been quite crude. Throughout the biblical period, communicating even in the most basic way would have been difficult and frustrating for a deaf person. Friendships, romance, work, and even leisure might have been next to impossible. Of course, the problems of a person born deaf or whose hearing failed early in life would be greater than those who became deaf late in life. Even with people who became deaf later in life, the deprivation was frustrating. 2 Samuel recounts the plight of Barzillai, who became deaf by the age of eighty. He laments that he cannot hear the sound of people singing (2 Samuel 19:35). The passage suggests he greatly missed hearing music.

The Old Testament writers, especially in the wisdom literature, emphasized the importance of hearing for learning and maturing. The willingness to listen and to hear instruction was considered a sign of personal growth. "Hear, my child, your father's instruction, and do not reject your mother's teaching" (Proverbs 1:8). "My child, if you accept my words and treasure up my commandments within you, making your ear attentive to wisdom ... then you will understand the fear of the Lord" (Proverbs 2:1-5). One gained wisdom and received instruction through the sense of hearing. No alternative is mentioned for those who cannot hear. Perhaps that lacuna suggests how marginalized were those unable to hear.

The way the Old Testament uses language suggests that hearing was integral to one's relationship to God. One of the key verses of the Old Testament was the "Shema," in Deuteronomy 6. "Hear, O Israel: The Lord is our God, the Lord alone" (Deuteronomy 6:4).

The name of the verse comes from the Hebrew word for "hear," which also means, "obey." Truly to hear the word of God was to obey. Other passages reinforce this idea. The psalmist contrasts making an offering with true obedience and uses the ear as a metonym for that obedience, "You have given me an open ear" (Psalm 40:6). Conversely, to disobey God was to shut one's ears. Jeremiah complains about the stubbornness of the people by saying, "their ears are closed, they cannot listen" (Jeremiah 6:10). Again, as in the wisdom literature, no provision is made for people who cannot hear. The language itself seems to exclude hearing-impaired people.

The ability to speak also is crucial for human interaction and one's relationship with God. The psalmist, who wants to think of a terrible punishment for himself if he forgets Jerusalem, picks the inability to speak as a fate he wishes to avoid (Psalm 137:6). It should be noted that the psalmist is a musician, and would therefore be unable to sing if his tongue stuck to the roof of his mouth. When the psalmists want to offer praise to God, they often wish their praises to come out as "singing" (see Psalm 108:1). Not only praise, but also a variety of interactions with God depend on the ability to speak. The psalmists cry to God (Psalm 120:1, 130:1), bless God (Psalm 134:1) and give thanks to God (Psalm 138:1). All of these forms of interaction require, if not the power of speech, at least the use of language. We can only surmise how people in the ancient world developed any ability to use language if they were born deaf. Psalm 103:1 suggests that the psalmists understood that a person could bless God with more than the organs of speech. He wants "all that is within" him to bless the Lord. Nevertheless, the power of speech was so important that one Old Testament scholar declares, "Thus the mouth, which expresses what ear and eye had perceived, becomes the organ which distinguishes man above all other creatures."[1]

None of the statements in this section should be understood as suggesting that deaf people are to blame for their condition or to suggest that deaf people lack faith or maturity or wisdom. I include this background material to highlight the problems and deprivation that deaf and hearing-impaired people experienced in the ancient world. In a sense, with limited ability to interact with others, learn, or practice their faith in God, they had to fight for their very humanity.

Literary Analysis

Jesus is once again in Gentile territory. Even though his first miracle among the Gentiles led to the people asking him to leave (5:17), Jesus' fame has spread so that he cannot get away from the people (7:24). The real heroes of the story remain anonymous. An indefinite "they" bring the deaf man to Jesus. We do not know if the ones who bring the man to Jesus are his family, his friends, or just concerned bystanders who have caught the buzz about Jesus. Because the narrator does not tell us that they are family or friends, perhaps the most likely possibility is that they are people who notice the deaf man and take him to Jesus. Their compassion shows through in what they do. They become the ears and mouth for the man who cannot hear about Jesus as the woman with the hemorrhage could (5:27) and cannot ask for Jesus' help as Jairus could. The narrator does not tell us explicitly that Jesus noticed their faith as he does with regard to that of the four men who bring the paralytic (2:5), but surely, their faith is exemplary, especially since they are Gentiles. We know precious little about the man himself. Apparently he was not born deaf, because he can speak some, just not clearly (the Greek in v. 32 suggests this). We don't know how long he had been deaf, or what hardships his deafness caused him.

The focus in the story is on Jesus' actions in healing. Jesus' actions are consistent with those of other ancient healers, suggesting that Mark shows us Jesus' superiority over them. Spitting and sighing are common to ancient healing stories. Saliva was thought to have healing qualities. The sighing could mean a number of things. Jesus could be expressing for the man his grief, or he could be drawing on God's power for the healing. As in some of the other healing stories, this account contains the language of exorcism: the man's tongue was "released" (v. 35).

Once again, Jesus orders the crowd ("them" in v. 36?) not to tell anyone about the healing. Even though Jesus has taken the man away by himself for the healing, the crowd can see the effect.

92

The admonishment to silence is again a signal to Mark's readers. Even though this story has great theological significance, the true understanding of Jesus has not come yet. The next chapter begins to unfold that significance as Jesus tells the disciples about his crucifixion and calls for them to take up their own crosses. We note, of course, that the crowd ignores the admonition to silence and begins to proclaim the message.

The crowd gets the last theological word, as has often been the case in these stories. They are astounded at the healing, declaring, "He has done everything well; he even makes the deaf to hear and the mute to speak" (v. 37). This declaration is an acknowledgment that healing the deaf is unique to Jesus. Jesus has done what Old Testament prophets and other healers of the ancient world had not done.

Theological Reflection

When the crowd exclaims that Jesus has "done everything well" (v. 37) we hear echoes of the creation story from the first chapter of Genesis, where God declares repeatedly that the creation and all of its parts are "good" (Genesis 1:4, 10, 12, 18, 21, 25, 31). [Note the Greek of Genesis 1 in the Septuagint contains some of the same vocabulary of Mark 7:37. Both use the words *panta* (all) and a form of *kalos* (good).] This narrative, therefore, links Jesus' healings with God's act of creation. The opening of a man's ears, and the restoration of the power to speak are appropriate for such a connection.

In the first creation story in Genesis, God creates through the power of speech, "Then God *said*, 'Let there be light' " (Genesis 1:3). The text, of course, does not say who heard God speak, only that speech was the instrument through which God created. Immediately after God spoke, what God commanded came into being, "and there was light" (v. 3). Such is the power of language in God's mouth.

In a couple of places, the Old Testament writers affirm that God created the ability to hear and the ability to speak. When the Lord appeared to Moses in a burning bush, calling him to lead the

93

Hebrew people out of slavery in Egypt, Moses offered several protests. Moses claimed to be "slow of speech and slow of tongue" (Exodus 4:10). The Lord's response was, "Who gives speech to mortals? Who makes them mute or deaf, seeing or blind? Is it not I, the Lord? Now go, and I will be with your mouth and teach you what you are to speak?" (Exodus 4:11-12). The Lord grants the power of speech in the general sense and will specifically teach Moses how to speak. The power of speech was integral to the very formation of the community of Israel, and to God's plan for them. The sages of Israel affirm, "The hearing ear and the seeing eye — the Lord has made them both" (Proverbs 20:12). This verse celebrates that our senses are a special gift from God.

We cited Isaiah 35:5-6 in the passage about the paralyzed man in Mark 2. "Then the eyes of the blind shall be opened, and the ears of the deaf unstopped; then the lame shall leap like a deer and the tongue of the speechless sing for joy." This passage proclaims that the healing of disabilities will be a sign of God's favor during the special event of the return from exile. The passage is an eschatological promise of God's blessing.

Given the importance of hearing and speech in biblical theology, the account of the deaf man in Mark takes on a special significance. This is more than a story about one man whose ears are opened. This is a proclamation that in Jesus, God is renewing creation. Jesus is restoring the goodness of creation corrupted by sin, illness, and demonic forces.

That the man Jesus heals of deafness is a Gentile is no accident. The man is both the recipient of God's gracious healing through Jesus and a synecdoche. He represents the Gentiles, to whom the word of salvation is preached. God is unstopping the ears of the Gentiles so that they can hear the good news. This speaks to us of the universality of the gospel message, and urges the church to proclaim the good news to all.

Pastoral Reading
Not many of us will face the prospect of being paralyzed, blind, or having a hemorrhage for twelve years. Loss of hearing, however, is a common problem that accompanies growing older. Sooner

94

or later, most of us will face the growing isolation of hearing impairment. We will be deprived of the beautiful sounds of music playing, birds chirping, and children laughing. Improvements in technology will help mitigate this situation somewhat, but the problems remain. Of all the healing stories, this may be the one that more of us will turn to for comfort and courage at some point in our lives.

One of the most painful aspects of deafness for some elderly people is the loss of full participation in church. People find the sermon hard to follow or the music difficult to enjoy. They can't keep up with conversations when someone speaks to them. They can't keep up in Sunday school. I have sat in the homes of many elderly parishioners who told me that they stopped going to church when their hearing became bad. They missed church terribly, but it was just too awkward and frustrating to keep going.

If we want to expand the range of people who might be able to identify with these healing stories, we might consider how they apply to people other than those who have the specific condition mentioned in the story. People who are shy are not addressed in scripture much (if at all). Even though they can hear perfectly, they may still feel left out of conversations and social situations. They may relate well to the feelings of isolation, loneliness, and frustration that a deaf person feels. This passage can provide a pastoral word to those who are shy or who have some condition such as social anxiety or Asperger's autism. God may open up channels of communication for them. In a variety of ways, God may loosen their tongues.

Needless to say, the church should do all it can to provide for the needs of the deaf and hard of hearing in all of its ministries. Sign language interpreters, special amplifiers, and provision for good acoustics are ways the church can show love and care to persons with hearing impairment. The ability to worship, interact with others, and take part in the life of the church is vital to all people.

The language we use is especially important in dealing with those who have trouble speaking. The old phrase "deaf and dumb" should be tossed away. The implications of "dumb" — because of the modern meaning of the term — are just too painful and insulting. Let us use patience and sensitivity when we speak of people with handicapping conditions.

The anonymity of the people who bring the deaf man to Jesus is instructive. That Mark doesn't identify them suggests that the details about them are not important. Let us do our work for the church without seeking attention or credit for ourselves.

Over and over, Jesus admonishes people not to tell about his miracles. Over and over, the people so admonished ignore Jesus' command and proclaim the message anyway. Even Jesus' miracles are not self-interpreting. Some of Jesus' opponents saw the miracles firsthand, but did not comprehend God's power in them. The Gospel of Mark opens by announcing the "good news" of Jesus Christ (Mark 1:1). The overall message of Mark is that once we truly understand the mission of Jesus, cross and all, we should proclaim the good news. Just as Jesus' miracles are not self-interpreting, neither are the church's actions. The role of proclamation is indispensable.

Preaching Strategies

Even though this passage is brief, it is rich in sermon potential. By focusing on different characters or different theological affirmations in the passage, the preacher can find material for several sermons. Although the characters in this story are not especially well developed, their actions are instructive for the church.

A focus on the people who bring the deaf man to Jesus reminds the church of its mediating role between Jesus and the world. In the text, the ones who bring the deaf man to Jesus are not necessarily followers of Jesus. They are not the disciples, who usually represent the church in Mark. Nevertheless, they recognize Jesus as a healer, and bring the man to him. Part of the church's mission is to communicate to a needy world the grace offered by Christ. The church takes the initiative to offer and interpret the grace of God. The church discerns the needs of the world and how the grace of Christ addresses that need. That discernment is important because people's perceived needs are not always their real needs.

The man in the story might not have known that Jesus could heal him.

The deaf man is a reminder to Christians that others have mediated the gospel to us. Perhaps someone shared a testimony with us. Maybe a Sunday school teacher or youth director made an impression on us. All Christians owe a debt to others who have preserved the church's witness through the centuries, sometimes at great cost.

The deaf man also reminds us that we are all recipients of grace. Because he might not have realized what would happen to him when he encountered Jesus, he personifies the unexpected joy of receiving grace. Many people have experienced the grace of God when they were not looking for it, or were even intentionally closed to it. God's grace finds us, even when we don't want to be found.

The deaf man is a synecdoche for human isolation. Even with the physical ability to communicate and the impressive technology that makes communication possible, we often feel estranged and lonely. Sometimes we cannot find the words to say to each other, even when we desperately want to communicate.

As is true with each of the miracle stories the healing itself points to a larger theological affirmation. Jesus' ministry is the coming near of the renewal of creation. Because Jesus does all things well he begins the process of restoring the creation to the goodness God intended. Part of that restoration is giving back the ability to enjoy the beauty of the creation and genuine fellowship with one another.

Kathy Black's book, *A Healing Homiletic: Preaching and Disability*[2], is an insightful book about preaching from the healing narratives in the New Testament. Part of her message is a caution about using physical disabilities as metaphors for sin and disobedience. Her book is instructive for all forms of disability but perhaps especially so for deafness. Mark intends this narrative about opening the ears of a deaf man to serve as a synecdoche for bringing the word to the Gentiles. As the man's ears are opened, so are the ears of the Gentiles opened to the proclamation of the word (7:36). Let us remember, however, that the inability to hear is not a good metaphor for the unwillingness to hear.

97

1. Hans Walter Wolff, *Anthropology of the Old Testament*, trans. Margaret Kohl (Philadelphia: Fortress Press, 1974), p. 77.

2. Kathy Black, *A Healing Homiletic: Preaching and Disability* (Nashville: Abingdon Press, 1996). Her chapter on deafness is especially helpful for understanding the needs of deaf people in contemporary society (pp. 88-103).

Miracle Nine

From Beggar
To Follower

The Text

*They came to Jericho. As he and his disciples and a
large crowd were leaving Jericho, Bartimaeus son of
Timaeus, a blind beggar, was sitting by the roadside.
When he heard that it was Jesus of Nazareth, he began
to shout out and say, "Jesus, Son of David, have mercy
on me!" Many sternly ordered him to be quiet, but he
cried out even more loudly, "Son of David, have mercy
on me!" Jesus stood still and said, "Call him here."
And they called the blind man, saying to him, "Take
heart; get up, he is calling you." So throwing off his
cloak, he sprang up and came to Jesus. Then Jesus said
to him, "What do you want me to do for you?" The
blind man said to him, "My teacher, let me see again."
Jesus said to him, "Go; your faith has made you well."
Immediately he regained his sight and followed him on
the way.*

Jesus' healing and exorcising ministry comes to an end with
this episode. After the healing of Bartimaeus, Jesus enters Jerusalem for the final confrontation with both the Judean and Roman
leaders. Of the Marcan healing/miracle narratives treated in this
book, this is the only one that takes place after the theologically
decisive chapter 8, where Jesus explains about his death. For that
reason, the healing of Bartimaeus' blindness has a symbolic meaning. Bartimaeus' words and actions in this narrative help us understand who Jesus is and how to respond to God's grace.

Background

Just as the ear enabled people to communicate, so the eye opened up the beauty of God's creation for people. For the Old Testament writers, the eyes were a gift bestowed by God. "The hearing ear and the seeing eye — the Lord has made them both" (Proverbs 20:12). The J-source writer used eyesight as a metaphor for deeper understanding, for recognition of an existential or theological truth. When Adam and Eve ate the fruit in the garden, "the eyes of both of them were opened, and they knew that they were naked" (Genesis 3:7).

Two poignant stories from the Old Testament help us appreciate the deprivation of blindness. In both stories, not only did the blind person lose the ability to appreciate what the senses can tell us, but also the loss of eyesight had implications for relationships and satisfaction from life itself. The story about the end of Isaac's life is well known. Because he is blind, his wife and son are able to take advantage of him. Rebekah and Jacob fool him into believing that Jacob is Esau, so that Jacob is able to steal Esau's blessing. Isaac's other senses work well, but he is still vulnerable because of his failed eyesight. He is unable to protect himself from the treachery of his own family (Genesis 27). In the second narrative, the priest, Eli, is Samuel's tutor. Eli is old and his eyesight has begun to fail. Eli is still able to help Samuel interpret God's call to him, but Eli's failing eyesight is a metaphor for his increasing ineffectiveness. He is unable to control his sons, Hophni and Phineas. He cannot provide spiritual guidance for the people of Israel in the struggle with the Philistines. At the end of his life, Eli sits by the side of the road: old, heavy, and blind. When he hears how badly the battle with the Philistines has gone and that his sons have been killed he falls over in grief, breaking his neck. A one-time spiritual leader dies in a pathetic, disgraceful way (1 Samuel 2-4).

Bartimaeus hails Jesus as "Son of David." This is the first time in the Gospel of Mark that this title has been used. David, of course, is the great king who united Israel, established Jerusalem as the capital, and expanded Israel's territory. The prophets proclaimed a time when the Davidic empire would be restored. Jeremiah prophesied to the exiles that the Lord would restore Israel and Judah and bring them back to the land. Centuries after the time of the great king, Jeremiah promised, "On that day, says the Lord of hosts, I will break the yoke from off his neck, and I will burst his bonds, and strangers shall no more make a servant of him. But they shall serve the Lord their God and David their king, whom I will raise up for them" (Jeremiah 30:8-9). Isaiah promises, "a shoot shall come out from the stump of Jesse" (Isaiah 11:1). In this prophecy, the leader who springs from the stump of Jesse (David's father) will usher in a time of justice, righteousness, wisdom, and even harmony in nature (see also Jeremiah 33:14-16). Those who, in Jesus' time, remained of ancient Israel still clung to this expectation that God would send a leader to restore the glory of David's time. Bartimaeus is the first character in the Gospel of Mark to make this connection with Jesus. This passage, however, reinterprets the coming of the Davidic messiah. No one expected the Davidic messiah to be a healer, but rather a warrior and ruler. Because Jesus did not lead an armed revolt against Roman imperialism, he did not fit the expectations of the people. Nevertheless, because Jesus can heal and vanquish the demonic forces he is a liberator. When Mark places the term "Son of David" on Bartimaeus' lips he asserts the political implications of Jesus' ministry. The time of liberation and salvation has begun. The breaking in of the dominion of God is a judgment on all human political structures. Bartimaeus' call to Jesus as "Son of David" was a challenge to the Judean officials and the Roman government.

Literary Analysis

It is instructive to compare the healing of Bartimaeus with the healing of a blind man in Bethsaida in chapter 8. The curious feature of that account is that Jesus seems to need two attempts to heal the man. Jesus puts saliva on his hands, lays his hands on the man, and then asks the man if he can see. The man can see somewhat but not clearly. His cryptic remark is that he "can see people, but they look like trees walking" (8:24). Jesus then lays his hands on the man's eyes again. After the second application the man can see. The placement of these two healing stories is important. The first story comes just before Jesus tells his disciples about his crucifixion. The second story comes after that announcement and just before Jesus goes to Jerusalem. The first story suggests that at this point in the Gospel of Mark, one can understand Jesus only partially. Jesus has been revealed only as the healer and exorcist who brings near the dominion of God. That is an important part of Jesus' identity but it is an incomplete understanding of Jesus. Bartimaeus, in chapter 10, can see clearly the first time. Mark may be saying that now, as Jesus and the disciples enter Jerusalem, we can see Jesus in his full identity as the healer who dies on the cross. In the verses just before the Bartimaeus story, Jesus defines himself as a servant. "For the Son of Man came not be served but to serve, and to give his life a ransom for many" (10:45). The healing of Bartimaeus is the signal that now the eyes of the disciples, and the reader, will be opened to who Jesus is.

Bartimaeus is a case study in assertiveness! When the crowd tries to shush him, he cries out even more loudly. As has been the case with the others Jesus has healed, Bartimaeus has little to lose and everything to gain by crying out. Nevertheless, we admire his courage. That Bartimaeus has heard of Jesus indicates that Jesus' fame has spread even to a person considered to be in the lowest social stratum, a beggar. Bartimaeus has probably had himself positioned in a high-traffic area so as to attract the most money. As Jesus and his entourage are leaving Jericho (after what must have been an uneventful visit, v. 46), Bartimaeus is in the right place at the right time. He sees his opportunity and takes it. The various crowds in the healing stories have played different roles. They sometimes help and sometimes hinder the person who needs healing. Here, the crowds try to silence Bartimaeus, but we don't know the reason. Perhaps their reaction to Bartimaeus indicates his lowly social status. Once Jesus calls Bartimaeus, the crowd changes its stance and tells him to "take heart." Bartimaeus' act of throwing off his cloak is a sign of his confidence that Jesus will grant his request.

Jesus' question to Bartimaeus is curious (v. 51). Surely Jesus knows he is blind. Jesus can read people with precision (2:8). Perhaps Jesus' question is a recognition that we all have multiple needs. Bartimaeus' answer suggests that he has not been blind from birth.

Bartimaeus is quite a contrast to the rich man who comes to Jesus earlier in the chapter (10:17-22). That man is rich; Bartimaeus is a beggar. That man can come to Jesus; Bartimaeus is lucky Jesus passed by. That man asks only for something after this life; Bartimaeus wants his life to change now. That man turns away from Jesus; Bartimaeus becomes a follower. Once again, Mark tells us that our need affects how we respond to Jesus.

Mark does not tell us what happened to the other characters who are healed. Bartimaeus becomes a follower. Mark lets us know that the real purpose of healing is to make followers of Jesus. Bartimaeus follows Jesus into Jerusalem, where Jesus will face the cross.

Theological Reflection

Repeatedly, Jesus (or the narrator) has commented on the faith of a person being healed or on the faith of those connected with the one healed. Certainly, Jesus is justifiably gratified when the people who come to him have faith. The question is what role faith has in the healing itself. Jesus heals people in cases where no mention of faith is made (1:40-45, where the man later disobeys Jesus). In his hometown, Jesus "could do no deed of power," presumably because of their "unbelief." (Mark says only that Jesus was "amazed at their unbelief," but Matthew is explicit that Jesus did not do many deeds of power there, because of their unbelief.) When Jesus raises Jairus' daughter, he exhorts Jairus "do not fear, only believe." We do not know if Jairus should "believe" to keep himself from despair, or because belief would facilitate the raising of his daughter. In some cases, Jesus assures a person that "your faith has made you well" (5:34, 10:52, see also 7:29). Taking all of the cases together, it seems safe to say that Jesus would not refuse to heal someone who had trouble removing all doubt or about whom Jesus was assured that the person would obey Jesus after the healing. Jesus' healing is a gracious gift, evidence that the dominion of God has come near. Jesus' comments praising the faith of people seem to be reassuring remarks to people who have overcome obstacles and impediments to get to Jesus. Certainly, Mark wants to encourage his readers to have faith and to persevere in seeking out Christ's power.

The Bartimaeus story introduces a new christological title for Jesus: Son of David. The first and most important title for Jesus is in Mark 1:1: Son of God. The title Jesus uses for himself is Son of Man. Although other titles are used for Jesus (such as teacher in 10:51, and prophet in 6:4), these three titles are the most significant in Mark's Gospel. Son of God, which the human community understands only at the foot of the cross (15:39), refers to Jesus' relationship to God. Jesus brings near the dominion of God. Son of Man can refer to the existential side of Jesus, the Jesus who will suffer and die (8:31) and to Jesus' authority over such things as the sabbath (2:28).[1] Son of David refers to the political aspect of Jesus' ministry. Jesus restores the Davidic kingship. Jesus does not oppose the Roman occupation in a military way, but serves as king by casting out demons and healing. Part of the job of a king was to protect and provide for his subjects. When Bartimaeus follows Jesus after having called him "Son of David" he is acting on his political loyalty. Jesus offers salvation and liberation that the Judean and Roman officials cannot.

In this story and in others, the word translated by the NRSV as "made you well" is the Greek word for "save," or "salvation." The popular misconception about salvation is that it has to do only with our "souls" after we die. The Greek word for soul as used in the New Testament does not refer to a disembodied "ghost" that lives on after we die. In biblical thinking, body and soul are inseparable. Salvation culminates in the liberation of the creation from its bondage (see Romans 8:21). Physical disabilities such as blindness and political corruption are manifestations of that bondage. Salvation refers to physical, spiritual, and cosmic wholeness. That wholeness begins now, in this life.

Pastoral Reading

I want to return to the discussion about the phrase, "your faith has made you well." On the one hand, we preachers want to encourage people to have faith, rather than to give in to despair. Faith can keep people courageous and hopeful even in the worst of situations. Nevertheless, the phrase "your faith has made you well" can have a downside. When people do not heal, the phrase Jesus uses can become a burden. People can believe that they have not gotten well because of their lack of faith. That can become a guilt trip. Additionally, such an attitude can make God seem cold-hearted. We can begin to believe that God waits up in heaven for us to muster enough faith. Trying to erase every shred of doubt can be a monumental task. A misunderstanding of this phrase can shift the responsibility for healing to our effort rather than God's grace.

In an article from the Internet, Daniel Yee writes about a study done on the effect of "optimism" on the survival rates of cancer patients. The patients in the study had the same form of lung cancer. The study found that optimism or a positive attitude made no difference in survival rates. Furthermore, the study suggested that trying to be optimistic became a burden. Patients believed that they had to conceal their true feelings in order to maintain optimism. Optimism did help some patients in other situations lead a better quality of life, and make healthy lifestyle choices.[2] Might not the same phenomenon apply to our exhortations to people to "have faith?" Having faith does not necessarily mean that we do not experience down times, times when we need to be honest with our frustration, and times when we need to ventilate our feelings. Faith can be continued trust in God even when hope for a "cure" has faded away.

The only experience I have had pastoring a person who was completely blind was in a hospital setting, and I did not have much contact with the patient. I have been pastor to people who encountered vision impairment. Cataracts, macular degeneration, and glaucoma are common problems. Many parishioners have expressed to me their frustration at not being able to drive or read. Their freedom and their ability to learn were both limited. Some of them wanted to lead in worship — to serve as a lector — but could not do so. Some them had trouble following the liturgy in the bulletin or reading the hymns. Kathy Black explains with sensitivity that blind people are forced to trust others without being quite sure whom they can trust.[3] The church should be on the forefront of addressing the social, worship, and employment needs of blind people.

Preaching Strategies

As the last of the healing stories in Mark, this passage helps us interpret all of the preceding stories. Mark has given the reader only meager information about how the other people healed by Jesus have responded. Simon's mother-in-law served Jesus and the others in her house. The leper in 1:40-45 went out proclaiming the word even though Jesus had admonished him not to say anything. The crowds who witness the healings often respond in wonder and amazement (see 5:42). In the Bartimaeus story, Mark pushes the reader to a proper understanding of the expected response to the grace, power, and healing offered by Jesus. The real contribution of this passage to the cycle of miracle stories in Mark is the emphasis at the end of the passage on Bartimaeus following Jesus. All of the miracle stories in Mark lead to this one. The appropriate response to Jesus' grace is to follow. As Simon's mother-in-law and the leper demonstrate, proclamation and service are part of that following. A sermon from this passage can move from the grace offered by Jesus to the discipleship modeled by Bartimaeus.

A sermon on this passage can reflect the irony that has run through all of the healing stories in Mark. That irony is that Jesus, the healer and life-giver, will be crucified. Chapter 11 begins Jesus' approach to Jerusalem, the place of his death. When Bartimaeus follows Jesus he follows to Jesus' death. If we can safely assume that having his eyesight restored enabled Bartimaeus to reclaim his previous life and employment, the irony is that he now risks his newfound life by following Jesus. Jesus has called his disciples to take up their crosses (8:34-38). Another irony is that Jesus has cautioned his followers in chapter 9 to tear out an eye if it causes them to stumble (9:47). Jesus is calling his followers to accept the values of the dominion of God. The dominion of God includes health and wholeness, but pursuit of that dominion sets up a conflict with the demonic forces of the world.

The preacher can move from an announcement of the gospel as gift — health and wholeness — to an announcement of the gospel as demand — discipleship and conflict with the demonic forces. Research studies have indicated that such things as church attendance and prayer can lead to longer life.[4] That is part of the gift of the gospel. We should not simply accept the gift of good health. We are called to respond by living sacrificial lives in confrontation with the evil of the world.

A sermon on this passage can exposit the implications of Bartimaeus calling Jesus "Son of David," a political term. If we look at the description of what the offspring of David will accomplish politically (Isaiah 11:1-5) we have an affirmation of the church's mission in advocating for the role of government in caring for the poor and meek.

1. Jack Dean Kingsbury, *The Christology of Mark's Gospel* (Philadelphia: Fortress Press, 1983).

2. Daniel Yee, "Optimistic attitude provides no help against cancer," Associated Press Archive <www.apdigitalnews.com/aparchive.html>, February 13, 2004.

3. Kathy Black, *A Healing Homiletic: Preaching and Disability* (Nashville: Abingdon Press, 1996), p. 59.

4. Chester L. Tolson and Harold G. Koenig document in their book, *The Healing Power of Prayer* (Grand Rapids: Baker Books, 2003), the positive effects of prayer on stress and the immune system.

Miracle Ten

Leftover Grace

The Text

After this Jesus went to the other side of the Sea of Galilee, also called the Sea of Tiberias. A large crowd kept following him, because they saw the signs that he was doing for the sick. Jesus went up the mountain and sat down there with his disciples. Now the Passover, the festival of the Jews, was near. When he looked up and saw a large crowd coming towards him, Jesus said to Philip, "Where are we to buy bread for these people to eat?" He said this to test him, for he himself knew what he was going to do. Philip answered him, "Six months' wages would not buy enough bread for each of them to get a little." One of his disciples, Andrew, Simon Peter's brother, said to him, "There is a boy here who has five barley loaves and two fish. But what are they among so many people?" Jesus said, "Make the people sit down." Now there was a great deal of grass in the place; so they sat down, about five thousand in all. Then Jesus took the loaves, and when he had given thanks, he distributed them to those who were seated; so also the fish, as much as they wanted. When they were satisfied, he told his disciples, "Gather up the fragments left over, so that nothing may be lost." So they gathered them up, and from the fragments of the five barley loaves, left by those who had eaten, they filled twelve baskets. When the people saw the sign that he had done, they began to say, "This is indeed the prophet who is to come into the world."

When Jesus realized that they were about to come and take him by force to make him king, he withdrew again to the mountain by himself.

When evening came, his disciples went down to the lake, got into a boat, and started across the lake to Capernaum. It was now dark, and Jesus had not yet come to them. The lake became rough because a strong wind was blowing. When they had rowed about three or four miles, they saw Jesus walking on the lake and coming near the boat, and they were terrified. But he said to them, "It is I; do not be afraid." Then they wanted to take him into the boat, and immediately the boat reached the land toward which they were going.

The Gospel of John does not have a year in the lectionary cycle. Passages from John are scattered throughout the three-year cycle. Because of this piecemeal approach to John congregations may not get a full understanding of John as a complete narrative. The preacher may need to help the congregation place the readings from John in context. For example, this passage refers to Jesus' previous signs (6:2). The preacher may need to refresh the congregation's memory about the earlier signs in John (such as turning water into wine in ch. 2 and the healing of the son of the royal official in ch. 4).

The remarks below will concentrate on the first of the two miracles in this passage: the feeding of the multitude. It is the better developed of the two incidents. Some of the information provided above concerning the stilling of the storm in Mark 4 may be helpful in studying the narrative of Jesus walking on the water in John 6.

Background
In both of the Genesis creation accounts, God provides abundant food for sustaining human and animal life. Genesis 1:29 designates plants and fruit as food for people. In Genesis 2:9, the first act of the Lord God on behalf of the newly created human is to plant a garden for food. The plants in the garden provide good food that is pleasing to the eye. Part of God's good creation is a supply of easily attainable food.

110

The initial act of disobedience in Genesis involves eating. The man and woman both eat of the fruit of the tree of the knowledge of good and evil (Genesis 3:6). The consequences of people eating the wrong thing were far-reaching. The punishment to the man for disobeying God was estrangement from the abundant and attainable food. Obtaining food became a frustrating struggle (Genesis 3:17-19). The Genesis accounts convey the necessity of food for people, God's will to provide it and the deprivation of food people experience in the fallen creation.

Later biblical writers continue the theme of deprivation of food as part of the fallen nature of the creation. They often interpret famine or hunger as God's judgment or as an indication of the alienation between humanity and creation (Ezekiel 14:21; Deuteronomy 28:48). In one narrative, hunger drove a mother to eat her son, an act bordering on the total loss of decency and humanity (2 Kings 6:24-29).

During Israel's wilderness experience after the exodus from Egypt, the Lord provided food for the journey. This food was a response to the complaints of the people. Each morning the Lord provided "manna" on the ground. Each evening quail covered the camp. The regularity and abundance of the food were manifestations of God's providence. The Lord instructed the people to trust that the Lord would appear each day. Following the Lord's instructions about how much to gather, and gathering enough for two days before the sabbath, were tests of the people's obedience. The purpose of the experience of receiving the food was to enable the people to acknowledge the identity of the Lord (Exodus 16).

The Babylonian exile was marked by hunger and deprivation. Lamentations expresses the anguish of the ones left behind in Jerusalem. A desperate search for food is one of the agonies of that time (Lamentations 1:11, 19; 2:12, 19). Once again, hunger drives the inhabitants of Jerusalem to cannibalism (2:20). The Lord's action to restore the Judeans to their land is depicted as a time of abundant food (Isaiah 49:9; Amos 9:13-15).

2 Baruch 29:8 identifies a reappearance of the manna from heaven as a sign of the eschaton. This passage was likely written at approximately the same time as the Gospel of John or shortly

afterward. It may, nevertheless, express ideas that predated the writing of John.

One of the works attributed to Elisha was the miraculous feeding of 100 men with twenty barley loaves and some grain. This narrative follows Elisha's act to make fresh a pot of stew that had spoiled. Both acts took place during a famine. God acted through the prophet to provide adequate food (2 Kings 4:38-44, see also 1 Kings 17:1-16 for a story about Elijah enabling a woman and her son to survive a famine).

All three of the synoptic gospels contain a parallel to this story (Matthew 14:13-21; Mark 6:30-44; Luke 9:10-17). John has either changed many of the details in the story or has used a different source from the synoptics. In John, the incident takes place on a mountain. In John, Jesus initiates the discussion of how to feed the crowd. Only John includes the detail of the boy having food. Only in John does Jesus test Philip.

Literary Analysis

Chapter 6 does not fit within the storyline of the Gospel of John. In chapter 5 Jesus is in Jerusalem. John does not say why he is on the Sea of Galilee at the beginning of chapter 6. Chapter 7 implies that Jesus has just left Judea for Galilee. Many scholars have proposed rearranging chapters 4-7 to make a better fit. Instead of such speculation perhaps we should read John as we have it. The final editor of John likely had a theological purpose in placing these chapters the way they are.

With several details about time, setting, and action the narrator associates Jesus with Moses. Jesus has just crossed a body of water as Moses crossed the Sea of Reeds (Exodus 14; John 6:1). The event is a time of testing as was the wilderness wandering (John 6:6; Deuteronomy 8:2). The feeding takes place at Passover, an important prelude to the Lord's delivery of the people from Egypt (Exodus 11-13). Even the large crowd may be intended to evoke the large number of people who left Egypt. Only in John does Jesus perform the miracle on a mountain, perhaps an allusion to Moses on Sinai.

112

The conversation between Jesus and Philip follows a typical pattern in John. Throughout the gospel Jesus converses with people who don't "get it." Nicodemus doesn't understand about being born again or born from above (John 3). The woman at the well does not understand about the living water (John 4). Philip doesn't understand Jesus' question about the food (6:6-8). Philip interprets the situation concretely, calculating the amount of money needed to purchase food. As in the previous conversations between Jesus and other characters, John uses the dialogue to enable the reader to interpret the story. Jesus provides what the world cannot provide (see 14:27).

In the synoptic gospels, the disciples initiate the conversation about how to feed the crowd. In John, Jesus initiates the conversation. This difference is consistent with the portrayal of Jesus in John. Jesus knows about people and knows what will happen. Jesus is in charge of the situation.

The crowd is a mystery. They follow Jesus because they saw the signs. Do some among them need healing? Do they simply want to see Jesus perform another sign? Do they want to become disciples? The reader does not know exactly why they follow Jesus, especially if they have brought no food with them. The crowd is quite passive up through verse 14. They follow Jesus, do as they are told, and receive the food offered by Jesus. In verse 14 they finally speak, identifying Jesus as "the prophet who is to come into the world." This could be a reference to Deuteronomy 18:15-22, a promise that a prophet like Moses shall arise. In the Deuteronomy passage, the people are to heed the words of this prophet.

In verse 15, the passivity of the crowd ceases. They assume an active role in taking Jesus "by force to make him king." The crowd now assumes a hostile stance, seeking to force Jesus into a role he does not want. Even if, as some scholars suspect, this verse has been inserted into the text in a late redaction of John, in the form of John we have now the crowd misinterprets the miracle. One role of a king was to provide for the needs of the subjects (see Daniel 4:12). Jesus is not the king the people expect.

The storm at sea in 16-21 is an outbreak of the demonic forces. Perhaps they sense Jesus' power in the feeding. Jesus is master of the sea and the demonic forces it represents. Human misunderstanding and demonic resistance follow Jesus' feeding of the multitude to his ministry. Perhaps the demons do understand the significance of the feeding!

Theological Reflection

All four gospels employ eucharistic language in the depiction of the miraculous feeding. In John's account, Jesus gives thanks and distributes the food. As a whole, the Gospel of John neglects the sacraments. At the last supper, for instance, Jesus washes the disciples' feet instead of distributing bread and wine.

If John intends this story to convey a theology of the eucharist two important emphases stand out. One emphasis is that this incident involves genuine hunger. By having this story do so much of the interpretive work for the eucharist, John ties the sacrament more closely to human need. Sharing the eucharist together propels the church out into the world of concrete suffering. Another emphasis is that — in contrast to the last supper — more than just the disciples share in this meal. Jesus feeds a huge crowd. God offers overabundant grace to the church (represented by the disciples at the last supper) but also to the world. God offers grace indiscriminately. Jesus fed all of those present, not just those who were "good" or "worthy."

The interpretation of the feeding in 6:25-59 reveals the eschatological dimension of the miracle. Jesus is the "Bread of Life." The Bread of Life nourishes the church as it awaits and bears witness to the resurrection. Eternal life begins now but reaches fulfillment in the resurrection.

The miracles in the Gospel of John are "signs" pointing to Jesus' identity. This passage interprets Jesus as a new Moses. As the new Moses, Jesus constitutes the church as the people of God.

The incident on the water in 6:16-21 reveals deeper dimensions of Jesus' identity. By walking on the water while the sea is rough and the wind is blowing, Jesus asserts his authority over the forces of nature and even the demonic realm. By exclaiming to the frightened disciples, "It is I," Jesus claims divine authority. The Greek sentence "I am" recalls the YHWH in the Old Testament.

114

YHWH is rooted in the Hebrew verb "to be." Although scholars debate the exact translation of YHWH, some possibilities include "I am who I am," or "I will be who I will be." By placing the words "I am" in Jesus' mouth John identifies Jesus as part of the Godhead.

Pastoral Reading

Every pastor encounters people who do not have enough, whether the lack involves food, money, love, or something else. During the recession and economic hardship of the first few years of the twenty-first-century food pantries and soup kitchens were overwhelmed with the sheer number of people needing assistance. Some agencies reported that former supporters now appeared at their door as clients. Nearly two-thirds of the world experiences chronic malnutrition or starvation. Poverty produces hopelessness and exacerbates social problems such as alcoholism and domestic violence. People who receive too little love, often become bitter. People who do not receive enough love early in life seem to lose the capacity to accept love when someone tries to offer it. In the midst of this crying need, the preacher proclaims from this passage God's excess of grace. That grace motivates the church to meet people's needs. God's grace is a word of hope and encouragement to those who do not have enough.

Something about this passage evokes a curiosity in many people (preachers included) to know "what really happened" at the miraculous feeding. How did Jesus feed all of those people with so little food? A recurring "explanation" of this miracle is that the people in the crowd were inspired by the little boy's offer of the loaves and fish. They really had food all along but were reluctant to share it. When they saw the boy give up his food they broke down and shared as well. Such an "explanation" does not take seriously John's purpose in the passage. Jesus can do what is impossible by human means. Jesus restores the abundance of food before the fall (see Genesis 2). Jesus' actions recall the abundant manna during the wilderness wandering. Jesus is the bread of life. Attempts to discover a rational explanation for the miracle sell this passage short. As important as sharing is this passage goes much deeper than sharing. When we read this passage we should not try to figure out what happened historically. We should just hold out our hands to receive God's abundant grace.

Preaching Strategies

A preacher can treat this compelling text with at least four approaches. Each approach makes a legitimate connection with a concern of the text. I will call these four approaches concrete, existential, ecclesial, and eschatological.

In a concrete approach, the preacher can direct attention to the genuine physical hunger of the crowd in the narrative. John does not tell us why the crowd puts itself in the situation of being so far from a source of food. Whatever the reason they made themselves so vulnerable, they are hungry. Jesus takes the fish and barley loaves (food usually associated with the poor) and meets the material needs of a large group of people. A sermon taking the concrete approach to this pericope can call the church to take seriously the devastating hunger and deprivation of the world. According to an undated newsletter from "Bread for the World," one third of the population of sub-Saharan Africa is chronically malnourished (figures are for 2004). The AIDS pandemic exacerbates the situation because workers are too sick to tend the crops that might alleviate the hunger. Even if Americans do not face starvation, many people in this country are malnourished. A sermon taking a concrete approach to this passage can alert the church to the crisis and empower a response.

The existential approach to this passage might name other ways in which people feel deprived. The narrative describes an emptiness that Jesus fills to overflowing. Many people sitting in the pews feel emotionally empty. Although emotional deprivation is not as urgent as starvation, many people who have adequate material resources need a word of grace from the pulpit. God fills our emotional emptiness and meets our hunger for love.

The ecclesial approach to this passage encourages the church in its ministry to the world. The church often faces enormous obstacles to its ministry, often with meager resources. Not only does the church lack the money to do the ministry it needs to do but also sometimes congregations can struggle just to pay the bills. Beyond just the creative use of resources by members to stretch what they

116

have churches often find that more gets done, with only a little, than anyone could imagine. God works through the gifts we offer.

The eschatological approach to this text draws on the eucharistic allusions in the story. Theologians often speak of the eschaton as a messianic banquet. In the eschaton, everyone will have enough. This approach draws on the interpretation of the feeding offered in 6:25-40. Jesus is the "Bread of Life" (v. 35). The bread from heaven gives life to the creation (6:33). One purpose of the feeding was to encourage belief. Belief leads to eternal life (6:40). In the eschatological approach to the text, the preacher can interpret communion as a foretaste of the messianic banquet and as sustaining spiritual nourishment for our lives now.

Miracle Eleven

Interrupting
The Interruption

The Text

Now a certain man was ill, Lazarus of Bethany, the village of Mary and her sister Martha. Mary was the one who anointed the Lord with perfume and wiped his feet with her hair; her brother Lazarus was ill. So the sisters sent a message to Jesus, "Lord, he whom you love is ill." But when Jesus heard it, he said, "This illness does not lead to death; rather it is for God's glory, so that the Son of God may be glorified through it." Accordingly, though Jesus loved Martha and her sister and Lazarus, after having heard that Lazarus was ill, he stayed two days longer in the place where he was.

Then after this he said to the disciples, "Let us go to Judea again." The disciples said to him, "Rabbi, the Jews were just now trying to stone you, and are you going there again?" Jesus answered, "Are there not twelve hours of daylight? Those who walk during the day do not stumble, because they see the light of this world. But those who walk at night stumble, because the light is not in them." After saying this, he told them, "Our friend Lazarus has fallen asleep, but I am going there to awaken him." The disciples said to him, "Lord, if he has fallen asleep, he will be all right." Jesus, however, had been speaking about his death, but they thought that he was referring merely to sleep. Then Jesus told them plainly, "Lazarus is dead. For your sake I am glad I was not there, so that you may believe. But let us go to him." Thomas, who was called the Twin,

119

said to his fellow-disciples, "Let us also go, that we may die with him."

When Jesus arrived, he found that Lazarus had already been in the tomb for four days. Now Bethany was near Jerusalem, some two miles away, and many of the Jews had come to Martha and Mary to console them about their brother. When Martha heard that Jesus was coming, she went and met him, while Mary stayed at home. Martha said to Jesus, "Lord, if you had been here, my brother would not have died. But even now I know that God will give you whatever you ask of him." Jesus said to her, "Your brother will rise again." Martha said to him, "I know that he will rise again in the resurrection on the last day." Jesus said to her, "I am the resurrection and the life. Those who believe in me, even though they die, will live, and everyone who lives and believes in me will never die. Do you believe this?" She said to him, "Yes, Lord, I believe that you are the Messiah, the Son of God, the one coming into the world."

When she had said this, she went back and called her sister Mary, and told her privately, "The Teacher is here and is calling for you." And when she heard it, she got up quickly and went to him. Now Jesus had not yet come to the village, but was still at the place where Martha had met him. The Jews who were with her in the house, consoling her, saw Mary get up quickly and go out. They followed her because they thought that she was going to the tomb to weep there. When Mary came where Jesus was and saw him, she knelt at his feet and said to him, "Lord, if you had been here, my brother would not have died." When Jesus saw her weeping, and the Jews who came with her also weeping, he was greatly disturbed in spirit and deeply moved. He said, "Where have you laid him?" They said to him, "Lord, come and see." Jesus began to weep. So the Jews said, "See how he loved him!" But some of them said, "Could not he who opened the eyes of the blind man have kept this man from dying?"

Then Jesus, again greatly disturbed, came to the tomb. It was a cave, and a stone was lying against it.

Jesus said, "Take away the stone." Martha, the sister of the dead man, said to him, "Lord, already there is a stench because he has been dead for four days." Jesus said to her, "Did I not tell you that if you believed, you would see the glory of God?" So they took away the stone. And Jesus looked upwards and said, "Father, I thank you for having heard me. I knew that you always hear me, but I have said this for the sake of the crowd standing here, so that they may believe that you sent me." When he had said this, he cried with a loud voice, "Lazarus, come out!" The dead man came out, his hands and feet bound with strips of cloth, and his face wrapped in a cloth. Jesus said to them, "Unbind him, and let him go."

This passage records the final and most dramatic sign in the Gospel of John. To our surprise the incident is not recorded in any other gospel. Because it is unique to this gospel it is instructive for understanding John's theology.

This text appears twice in the three-year lectionary cycle. In year A the church reads the entire account of the narrative (vv. 1-45) on the fifth Sunday of Lent. In year B (the subject of this book) the lesson for All Saints is verses 32-44 of this chapter. The context of the reading might influence the interpretation. During Lent, the emphasis in the passage might be on the struggle between the forces of life and death in the passage. On All Saints' Day the emphasis might be on the raising of Lazarus as a precursor of the general resurrection. Despite the length of the passage, I will comment on the whole story from 11:1-44.

Background

One important background to this narrative in John is the theme of life running through the whole gospel. From the opening verses of the Prologue (1:1-18) the Gospel of John interprets Christ (the Word made flesh) as the source of life. "What has come into being in him was life, and the life was the light of all people" (1:3b-4). On one level the Gospel of John affirms the gift of life itself. The real emphasis in John is on quality of life or, in John's terms "abundant life" (10:10). The Gospel of John understands that existence in the world is difficult and that the church does its ministry in the world in a hostile environment (15:18-19). Nevertheless, the life Jesus offers is marked by peace (14:27), relationship with the risen Christ (15:5-7), and communal love (13:34-35). These qualities make life in the world abundant.

Part of the background to John's understanding of abundant life is the Old Testament wisdom tradition. John presents the divine word (*logos*) as an instrument in creation (1:3). In the biblical wisdom, tradition order was built into the creation. Recognition of the divine order in creation was a component of wisdom. Development of wisdom led one to fulfillment and harmonious relationships with others. Proverbs 8:22-36 is a poetic statement of this affirmation of wisdom theology. Verses 35-36 especially reflect the promise that wisdom influences the quality of life. "For whoever finds me finds life and obtains favor from the Lord; but those who miss me injure themselves; all who hate me love death." For John, a relationship with the risen Christ enables abundant life, even in the midst of hostility and persecution. The contrast between life and death in these verses from Proverbs helps us understand the conflict between life and death in John 11.

Another important theological term in the Lazarus narrative is "glory" (11:4, 40). The Hebrew term for glory (*kabod*) refers to weight or importance. To reveal God's glory is to make evident God's power, presence, and significance. In Exodus 16:7-10, the people see God's glory in a cloud that reveals God's presence. God's glory appeared later on Mount Sinai as a "devouring fire" (Exodus 24:17). In a bizarre and dramatic scene, Ezekiel declares that the glory of the Lord departed from the temple in Jerusalem. The glory of the Lord returns in chapter 43. The raising of Lazarus is a manifestation of the presence and power of God.

Literary Analysis
This narrative is quite rich. It is a relatively long piece, so John displays his artistic skill. It is filled with interesting characters, suspense, and dramatic tension.

Although we think of Lazarus as the "title" character in the story, he is really a flat character. He never speaks. His only acts are to become ill, die, and walk out of the tomb. His sisters interact with Jesus on his behalf. We infer from the narrator's affirmation that Jesus loved Lazarus and the grief of his sisters, that Lazarus was likable. Beyond those things, we know little about Lazarus. The plot of the story revolves around what happens to him, but he does not emerge as a developed character. By placing the emphasis on the sisters and on how Lazarus' death affects others, John focuses on the grief process in this passage. This story is not about fear or anxiety over our own deaths, but about how we grieve for the loss of those we love.

Lazarus' sisters, especially Martha, are the characters whose personalities are most well developed in the story. Early in the account they act as one character. The narrator attributes the sending of the message to Jesus to both sisters (11:3). When Jesus arrives on the scene the two women react differently. Martha comes out to meet Jesus while Mary stays in the house. The conversation between Martha and Jesus is poignant. The preacher must make interpretive decisions about this conversation. How should we understand Martha's comment to Jesus in verse 21? "Lord, if you had been here, my brother would not have died." Was she angry that Jesus had delayed? If she wasn't angry what emotion did she feel? Does her mood change by the next sentence (v. 22)? Is she holding on to a strand of hope? In this exchange, Martha seems to be caught between despair and hope. She is in despair that Jesus did not arrive in time, but continues to hope even after Lazarus' death. In verses 24-27 Martha affirms a future resurrection and confesses Jesus as the Messiah. Her grief does not undermine her faith. If she held any hope that Jesus could revive Lazarus in verse 22, she seems to have accepted the reality of his death by verse 39. As the church of today experiences death, Martha represents a positive Christian stance toward the death of a loved one. She accepts the death, anticipates future resurrection, and maintains faith in Jesus. Within the story she represents the "realistic" attitudes of the world. Jesus bursts through that "reality" by raising Lazarus.

Mary's response in the passage is less developed. In verse 32 she says essentially the same thing to Jesus as Martha does in verse 21 (the Greek is slightly different). She then continues weeping. If Martha demonstrates good theology, Mary shows understandable emotion. Many readers can identify with Mary, who seems to be too overcome with emotion to continue the conversation.

John reveals a side of Jesus that does not come out often. Early in the passage, Jesus is in total control of himself and the situation. When he hears of Lazarus' illness Jesus seems unaffected. He intentionally remains where he is and confidently interprets the illness as an opportunity to reveal God's glory. Jesus explicitly and firmly tells the disciples that Lazarus is dead (verse 14). He shows no fear of those who might kill him if he returns to Judea (verses 7-10). After Jesus' encounter with Martha and Mary he weeps. We may not know the exact cause of Jesus' tears, but the reader knows that Jesus is moved. Jesus may weep because of the accumulation of emotion. He grieves for Lazarus; he sees the sorrow of the sisters; he recognizes the lack of faith of his opponents. Jesus is more human and vulnerable in this passage that anywhere else in John. Issues of life and death touch us at the deepest level. Jesus himself is not exempt from these powerful emotions.

The disciples are a minor character in the passage. They attempt to discourage Jesus from returning to Judea (11:8) and misinterpret Jesus' words about Lazarus (11:12). Thomas emerges from the pack to suggest that the disciples should go with Jesus to Judea to die (11:16). Lazarus' illness could end up threatening the entire movement!

The crowd consoles Mary and witnesses the reanimation of Lazarus. Some within the crowd scoff, wondering why Jesus did not keep Lazarus from dying (11:37). The crowd connects this story with chapter 9 where Jesus heals a blind man. Those members of the crowd represent skepticism and doubt.

Lazarus' death is not the only issue in the passage. The disciples bring up the possibility of Jesus' death in verse 8. Thomas bravely volunteers the disciples to risk death. Immediately following the incident with Lazarus Jesus' opponents plot to kill him (11:53). In a sense, death is a character in the story. Death causes fear, grief, possibly anger (Martha), and doubt. Death appears to have triumphed. At the end of the story (v. 44), Jesus has won the victory over death. This conflict creates the tension and drives the plot of the story.

Jesus' delay, the misunderstanding of the disciples, Lazarus' actual death, the grief of the sisters, and scoffing of the members of the crowd all work to heighten the tension and suspense in the narrative. Jesus' task seems more difficult the further the story goes along. The process of decay of a dead body seems to deny the possibility that Jesus will be successful (v. 39). All of the forces arrayed against Jesus make his eventual triumph all the more dramatic.

Theological Reflection

John calls Jesus' miracles and healings "signs." The signs point to Jesus' identity and inculcate belief in Jesus. At the conclusion of the first sign, turning water into wine at Cana, Jesus' glory is revealed and the disciples believed in him (2:11). Nicodemus cites Jesus' signs as evidence of God's presence (3:2). Those who witnessed a sign did not necessarily believe in Jesus because of the sign. Jesus opponents do not believe in him even though they accept the validity of a healing. In chapter 5, Jesus heals a man on the sabbath. Jesus' opponents do not question the healing, but still seek to kill him. Even those who accept the signs as evidence of God's presence with Jesus do not fully understand Jesus' identity. Nicodemus misunderstands Jesus' teachings about being born again/from above (ch. 3). The crowd that has just eaten the miraculous meal provided by Jesus misinterprets his role as a king (6:15).

In this narrative in chapter 11, Martha correctly acknowledges Jesus' identity before she sees the sign. She declares Jesus to be "the Messiah, the Son of God, the one coming into the world" (11:27). Even after the sign, Jesus' opponents do not recognize Jesus for who he is. They consider him a nuisance and a troublemaker. They fail to believe even though they use the term "sign" themselves (11:47). One would have expected that this dramatic and impossible-to-refute sign would have convinced everyone of

Jesus' identity. Jesus' opponents and Judas do not come to belief even though they see the reanimation of Lazarus.

The term "believe" is a key concept in the Gospel of John. John tells us that the purpose of the book is to enable belief (20:31). John is not quite clear about the process of coming to belief in Jesus. The beloved disciple believed when he saw the empty tomb (20:8).[1] He seems to come to belief suddenly. John does not tell us if the beloved disciple decided to believe at that point or if the experience of belief was beyond his control. In other words, perhaps the sight of the empty tomb was so overwhelming that any doubt or unbelief was swept away. Thomas consciously chooses not to believe until he sees and touches the risen Christ (20:24). The signs are an inducement to belief but do not guarantee belief. Through the lips of Jesus, John praises those who believe even though they have seen none of the signs. From the evidence we can conclude that we have some choice in believing in Jesus.

John's understanding of belief includes intellectual assent to a correct understanding of Jesus' identity as the Son of God, but it really is a deep personal trust in Jesus. Belief is an antidote to fear (20:19). Belief empowers the disciples for ministry (20:21). Belief leads to eternal and abundant life (20:31). Belief in Jesus reveals God (12:44).

The reanimation of Lazarus demonstrates Jesus' power over death. It foreshadows Jesus' own resurrection. The grave clothes Lazarus wears in verse 44 mark the difference between Lazarus' experience and Jesus' resurrection. Jesus brings Lazarus back to life, but he continues in life as we know it. His body still bears the grave clothes. Jesus' resurrection is a transformation. Jesus passes through the grave clothes, which lie empty in the tomb (20:5-7). The two narratives together (Lazarus and Jesus' resurrection) make an important point in John's theology. Eternal life begins now for the believer. This is the emphasis in the Lazarus story. Jesus speaks in present tense, "I am the resurrection and the life" (11:25). Even so, the believer anticipates a resurrection after death (14:3, 11:24). John understands eternal life as both a "now" experience and a "not yet" reality.

Pastoral Reading

A fourth-year medical student named Ming He encountered a dying man on one of her rounds. A cancer patient, the man was only 26 years old. His agonizing words to her were, "Now that I am dying, I realize that I never really learned how to live."[2] This passage from John concerns the big issues of life and death. Jesus conquers the powers of death. Lazarus' illness seemed to rob him of life. Jesus restores that life. The words of the dying man in the hospital raise the more important issue of what we do with the life we have. Although the emphasis in the passage is on how Lazarus' death affects others, Lazarus is the one who gains more years of life. Given the anticipated joy of the resurrection we might even ask if Jesus did Lazarus such a favor. Eventually he will grow older and die again. He gains a few more years. What do those extra years mean?

In the Gospel of John, what we moderns call "quality of life" is a life lived in relationship with the risen Christ. When some of Jesus' disciples turn away, Jesus asks the remaining disciples if they will leave, also. Their answer is that only Jesus has the "words of eternal life" (6:68). The disciples could find an easier or safer life, but they experience eternal life in relationship with Jesus. The Gospel of John calls the church to ministry in a hostile environment. The world will "hate" the disciples (15:18). Despite this hostility John affirms that life in obedience to God is an abundant life (10:10). If Jesus grants Lazarus more years of life he will find those years most abundant if he lives them in relationship to the risen Christ and in obedience to God.

As stated above, this passage is about grief over the death of those we love. Every pastor has conducted heartbreaking funerals. My hardest two funerals were for a family that lost two infant children within a year and a half. Their grief was inexpressible. This passage promises that God triumphs over death. Even when we affirm the resurrection, the wait until we are reunited with our loved ones can be agony. For us, faith means continuing to trust in spite of our grief and questions about why. We are not granted what Mary and Martha receive: the immediate return of their brother. Our faith must be a durable faith.

Preaching Strategies

The movie, *Cold Mountain*, is set in the Civil War. One scene in the movie shows the two main characters, a young man and young woman, who are beginning a relationship, sitting in church. The congregation is singing a hymn about how life in the resurrection will be superior to life as we know it. In the middle of the hymn a man quietly enters the church to whisper something to another man. Before long the whispering increases. One by one people begin to rise from the pews and go outside. The last few congregants in the building finish the song, but then go outside. The men outside are shouting, backslapping, and throwing their hats in the air. They are celebrating the start of the war. In the scene from the movie a celebration of violence and death interrupts a celebration of the resurrection.

Death is always an interruption. Death interrupted the love between the characters in the movie. Death interrupts retirement plans. Death interrupts lives barely begun. War interrupts careers and family life. The preacher can name ways in which death interrupts life. The community may have experienced a sudden, tragic, or untimely death. The war in Iraq has led to over 1,500 deaths of young soldiers (at the time of this writing). Lazarus' illness was an interruption. We infer from the passage that he was a relatively young man, not expected to die.

Jesus interrupts the interruption. Death is a kind of malevolent power. Jesus conquers the power of death. Christians still mourn at the death of a loved one. The church comforts those who grieve. Our hope is in the resurrection, to which the reanimation of Lazarus points.

---

1. Most scholars think that the disciple whom Jesus loved was the founder of the Johannine community. See Raymond E. Brown, *The Community of the Beloved Disciple* (New York: Paulist Press, 1979).

2. Claudia Kalb, "Faith and Healing," *Newsweek* magazine, November 10, 2003, p. 44.

Contemporary Miracles, Healings, And Ministry

A book on preaching from the miracles should address the contemporary situation. I offer these modern day examples for your edification. I will list these illustrations in no particular order. I hope that in reading through them, preachers will find their own imaginations stimulated. In some cases, the connection to a particular text may seem obvious: a story about a blind man would easily fit the Bartimaeus narrative. Nevertheless, a preacher might find a creative way to fit an example about blindness into a sermon from a text that does not mention blindness. An example about AIDS might fit in with the passage about the leper (Mark 1:40-45), or with the passage about the woman with the hemorrhage (Mark 5:21-43). Read through these modern day accounts of people who have overcome despair, or found God's grace, or of the church's ministry to people with limitations, and let them enable your own reflection about our embodiment, the reality of the demonic and God's providence in the creation.

A Ministry To Children With Physical Limitations

Elissa Montanti, a former hospital lab assistant, runs a ministry for children who have lost limbs to violence, natural disaster, or birth defects. She began her work in the '90s when she found out about a fourteen-year-old boy who had lost three limbs to a land mine in Bosnia. With no money or connections, Montanti persuaded physicians, manufacturers of prosthetic limbs, politicians, and church groups to help her in her work. As of December 2003, Montanti's group, The Global Medical Relief Fund, had helped 35 children worldwide. She and her organization have brought children from Russia, El Salvador, Sierra Leone, Niger, Mexico, the Ivory Coast, Liberia, and Ghana to the United States for treatment. Her work requires her to face the demonic powers of war, despair, red tape, and apathy. She acknowledges that she gets by "on a shoestring and lots of prayer." When the struggle threatens to overwhelm her, she encourages herself with her success stories. "When

129

a child returns home with a new artificial leg and an enormous smile, nothing could be more gratifying." Her ministry has impressed others. One Bosnian official commented, "I was touched that an American woman would go to a God-forsaken town and hug kids with no arms or legs. Elissa has a big heart and endless energy."

Diane Hales, "One Child at a Time," *Parade* magazine, *The Dallas Morning News*, December 21, 2003, pp. 10-11. Website: <www.globmed.org>.

Miraculous Recovery From A Viral Infection Of The Brain

In August of 2001, Caroline Crouch lay near death in Children's Hospital in New Orleans. She had been brought to the hospital by helicopter while enduring body-jarring seizures. The physicians at Children's Hospital gave her little hope for survival. She was diagnosed with a viral infection, likely meningitis or encephalitis. Caroline had been placed on the prayer lists of several denominations. Her great-aunt, Ann Kay Logarbo, was a pediatrician. Dr. Logarbo's Catholic mother-in-law had suggested that the family seek the intervention of Blessed Francis Xavier Seelos, a nineteenth-century priest. Prayers to Father Seelos had possibly led to a woman being healed of cancer in 1966. In the wee hours of the morning of Caroline's third day in the hospital, Dr. Logarbo sought solitude for prayer. Her medical training led her to believe that only a miracle could save Caroline. During her prayer time she experienced a "fullness and a sense that God was speaking to me. And what he said was 'Get up and go see her.' " She went into Caroline's room, knelt by her bed and whispered that God would send her back to her family. She told Caroline to turn her head if she heard the whispers. Even though she was heavily sedated, Caroline turned toward Dr. Logarbo. That was the beginning of Caroline's recovery. The Vatican is researching the miracle to see if it enables Father Seelos to qualify for sainthood.

Bruce Nolan, "An Ailing Girl's Recovery May Offer Proof for Sainthood," *The Dallas Morning News*, February 7, 2004, p. 5G.

Prayers To Father Seelos For Cancer

The woman mentioned in the account above who was cured of cancer was named Angela Boudreaux. In 1966, Angela was diagnosed with liver cancer. Nineteen percent of her liver was affected, and the doctors predicted she would live no more than two weeks. In the words of one doctor, "She looked like someone out of a concentration camp." Despite her grim prognosis, Angela prayed to Father Seelos, asking to live so that she could raise her four children. Soon after the prayer, the doctors noticed that her tumor had begun to shrink. Her physician affirmed that her recovery could not be attributed to chemotherapy alone. A few months after her prayer, Angela was out of bed and caring for her children. In 2000, Angela was seventy years old, and attended the beatification of Father Seelos. The Roman Catholic Church has declared the healing a miracle.

Kenneth L. Woodward, "What Miracles Mean," *Newsweek* magazine, May 1, 2000, p. 57.

Recovery From Polio

In the 1940s, Walter and Marguerite Grounds watched anxiously as their fourteen-year-old daughter, Janet, was placed into an iron lung. On a Saturday she had complained of "feeling really bad." A local doctor's initial diagnosis was influenza. By Tuesday, her situation appeared grave, and the physicians realized that she had polio. Her hope for survival was slim. The disease was spreading through her limbs, diaphragm, and abdominal nerves and muscles. Walter lay awake that Tuesday night, praying Psalm 23 repeatedly. He had long practiced repetitive prayer, often using the Lord's Prayer. In defiance of the prognosis of the physicians, Janet began to recover. A few weeks after her admission, she began to regain neuromuscular control. Within a couple of months she was out of the iron lung. Then she went home. Within months she was back at school and had begun physical therapy. Her recovery was not medically impossible, but it was considered unlikely. Through it all, Walter's faith that his daughter would recover never wavered.

Harold G. Koenig, *The Healing Power of Faith: Science Explores Medicine's Last Great Frontier* (New York: Simon and Schuster, 1999), pp. 29-31.

Ministry To Unwanted Orphans

Christian Freedom International, a missionary group run by Jim Jacobson, a former political policy analyst, seeks to help orphaned children in Thailand and Myanmar. The children are refugees from the oppressive government of Myanmar. They are difficult to adopt because they do not have proper identification documents, such as birth certificates. The children number in the thousands, but as Jacobson says, "they are not on anyone's list." The United Nations and the Thai government have done little to help. Christian Freedom International builds schools and orphanages, raises money to provide food, and seeks to cut through red tape to help the children find adoptive families. Without intervention, the children would likely end up absorbed into the Thai sex industry. Lepers and the woman with the hemorrhage were also "not on anyone's list," but were welcomed by Jesus.

Rena Pederson, "Orphans Aided By Ministry," *Dallas Morning News*, May 22, 2004, p. 1G; website: <www.christianfreedom.com>.

Disabled Face Obstacles To Employment

According to the 2000 census, more than 43 percent of people with disabilities are unemployed. People with disabilities are almost twice as likely to be unemployed as able-bodied people. The median income for people with disabilities is $27,000, but able-bodied people earn a median income of $32,000. Carlene Strickland exemplifies the struggles of disabled people looking for jobs. She had twenty years of management experience before an automobile accident left her paralyzed. Despite her MBA, she has been unable to find a full-time job since her accident. Often, people with disabilities can perform the work, but run into problems with health insurance restrictions, transportation, and intransigent attitudes from employers. Some nonprofit organizations try to assist people with disabilities to find work. One such organization is REACH Resource Centers on Independent Living (website: www.reachcils.org). This center provides training, advice on creating resumes, and job interview practice. The church can support such organizations and be an advocate on behalf of people with handicapping conditions for such things as Social Security benefits, improvements in public transportation, and awareness of the quality work done by many people with disabilities.

Jennifer LaFleur, "Disabled Job Seekers Find Quandary Instead," *The Dallas Morning News*, April 19, 2004, p. 1A.

A Youth Healed Of Malformed Knees

Tyler Clarensau experienced a miraculous healing in 1999. Fourteen years old at the time, he attended a service at Park Crest Assembly of God Church in Springfield, Missouri. He had sought healing many times for his malformed knees. Surgery had not corrected the problem. At this service, Tyler was surrounded by forty other youth who began to pray for him. The whole congregation joined in the prayer. After an hour, a church leader decided that Tyler had been healed. The young man stood up and began to do deep knee bends, something he previously could not do. A year after the healing he could run, even if only slowly. In Tyler's words, "I'd heard stories about people getting healed, and I thought it was pretty cool. But I didn't really know for sure until it happened to me."

Kenneth L. Woodward, "What Miracles Mean," *Newsweek* magazine, May 1, 2000, p. 58.

Prevalence Of Mental Illness

Mental illness is often misunderstood. Many forms of mental illness have a physical component, such as chemical imbalances in the brain. People with mental illness still face a stigma from the mistaken belief that all mental illness is a moral or emotional failure. People are often afraid of those with mental illnesses. The church has a ministry to people with mental illnesses. That ministry includes support, advocacy, and pastoral care. A recent study found the incidence of mental illness high all around the world. In most countries, mental illness is under-treated. In various countries, between 36 and 85 percent of mental illness was untreated. One researcher commented, "In every country there is a hidden or unhidden stigma. People are reluctant to admit that they have mental problems" (quote attributed to Dr. T. Bedirhan Ustun of the

World Health Organization). The highest rate of mental illness was found in the United States. The researchers believe that part of the reason for the high incidence of mental illness in the United States is that people live with such high expectations of success that many people are frustrated.

Lindsey Tanner, "Study Says Mental Illness Prevalent Worldwide," AP AOL News, June 1, 2004.

A Caution About Looking For "Miracles"

Philip Hefner, professor of systematic theology at the Lutheran School of Theology at Chicago does not like the use of the term "miracles." He expresses problems with the idea that God contravenes the laws of nature. He cites as one mistaken example of looking for a miracle an incident in which a motel employee did not show up for work because her mother had had a vision that she should not go in. That night an intruder shot and killed three clerks at the motel. Hefner wonders why God would not want to save all four people. He does not say whether he believes that the mother really did have such a vision, or if she did what it meant. He raises important questions about God's intervention. For every miracle healing, there are many more stories of people who were not healed. All preachers who address the miracles must wrestle with such questions.

"Why I Don't Believe in Miracles," *Newsweek* magazine, May 1, 2000 p. 61.

A War Against Evil

Covenant House, a Roman Catholic ministry to runaway teenagers, reaches out to youth who have been kicked out of their homes, or caught up in the sex industry, or with a number of other needs. In a newsletter, Sister Tricia Cruise talks about how Covenant House rescued a seventeen-year-old girl from a sex slavery ring. The girl, Elisabeth, had managed to run away from her kidnappers, and found a woman who helped her phone their crisis line (1-800-999-9999). The people at Covenant House were able to rescue Elisabeth from a horrible fate. The newsletter refers to the woman who helped Elisabeth make the call as a "guardian angel." One paragraph from the newsletter reflects a modern understanding of the battle against demonic forces conveyed in Mark 1:21-28. "At Covenant House we have been at war with users of children since we first opened our doors thirty years ago. Every day we battle pimps and drug dealers who promise homeless children food and shelter, then threaten them, beat them, imprison them, and then use them for profit. We have won many, many battles with these criminals and saved thousands and thousands of lives." We cannot responsibly say that the pimps and drug dealers are "possessed by demons," but the drug and child sex industries are certainly demonic.

From a newsletter dated May 27, 2004.

A School For The Deaf In Liberia

David T. Worlobah runs a school for deaf students in Monrovia, Liberia. Not only does he teach the students to read, sign, and learn job skills, he also works in the community to change perceptions about persons with disabilities. In African society, persons with disabilities are considered useless and of little value. Sometimes, even the families of his students are not aware that deaf people can work and be productive. One especially poignant comment he made was that before coming to his school and learning language, many of his students did not realize that they had names. Worlobah finds real joy in his ministry. In his words, "Every time I see their faces, I see happiness, good future, and God's unconditional love."

Bill Fentum, "Deaf Liberians Gain Hope at School Founded by Mission Volunteer," *United Methodist Reporter*, 6.30 January 9, 2004, p. 2.

Backlash Against Anti-Drug Crusade

The Atlanta home of a minister, Reverend John Kimbrough, a crusader against drugs, was firebombed on June 6, 2004. Reverend Kimbrough was attending church at the time of the attack, and was not hurt. Shortly before the attack, he had held a meeting at his house to plan ways to combat drugs in the city. A suspected drug dealer was arrested at the scene. The incident reminds us of the ways in which the demonic forces resisted Jesus' ministry, especially the passage that describes the demonic forces of the sea trying to destroy Jesus and his followers (4:35-41). Although we would not say that drug dealers are "possessed" by demons, the drug trade — in its heartlessness and destruction of human lives — seems demonic (understood as that which opposes God's will).

Bill Gentum, "Pastor's House Burned After Drug-Traffic Arrests," *The United Methodist Reporter*, June 18, 2004, p. 2.

Soldier Blinded In Iraq

Jeremy Feldbusch was a strapping, athletic soldier when he joined the Army Rangers, and was deployed to Iraq. In April of 2003, Feldbusch and his platoon were guarding a strategic spot northwest of Baghdad when a shell burst close by. A piece of shrapnel entered his right eye and lodged in his brain. The fragment also damaged the optic nerve to his left eye. Back home in Pennsylvania, the former wrestler, football star, and champion weightlifter depends on his parents for nearly everything. The damage to his brain has made him moody, and the anti-seizure medication makes him tired. Not being part of a team has made Jeremy lonely. The experience has caused Jeremy to question why God would take his eyes. Despite his injury, Jeremy is moving toward acceptance. In his words, "I'm fine with it [the blindness] now. I'm going to learn Braille. I'm going to get a cane. I'll survive. There's more to life than seeing." Jeremy plans to start lifting weights again and to earn a master's degree.

Jeffrey Gettleman, "A Soldier's Return, to a Dark and Moody World," *The New York Times*, December 30, 2003, p. 1A.

Young Man With Muscular Dystrophy Shows Courage

Mattie Stepanek packed a whole lifetime into thirteen years. Even though he was severely disabled by Muscular Dystrophy, and needed a wheelchair and ventilator, he lived a courageous and joyous life. He wrote five books of poetry, three of which appeared on the *New York Times* best-seller list. Stepanek began writing poetry at the age of three to cope with his grief over the death of his brother, who also had Muscular Dystrophy. In addition to his poetry, Stepanek was a spokesperson for MDA. He counted among his acquaintances Jerry Lewis, Jimmy Carter, and Oprah Winfrey.

Mattie's website shares some of his inner thoughts. He writes that when he was angry, scared, or battling despair over his illness, prayer or time spent with family and friends pulled him through. He proclaims, "I am very blessed to have God and my mom so involved in my life." Elsewhere he says, "So my life is very difficult, and sometimes painful, but very full and blessed." What mattered to Mattie was the chance to make a difference in the lives of others. Mattie died from complications of his illness on June 22, 2004.

Website: <www.MattieOnline.com>.

An Exorcism Gone Wrong

A pastor in a storefront church in Milwaukee attempted to "exorcise" a demon from an eight-year-old boy who was autistic. The pastor of the church attributed the symptoms of autism to demons. The child died during the exorcism. Part of the exorcism involved holding the child down, with the pastor placing his knee on the child's chest, as well as lying on top of the child, chest to chest. The boy died of asphyxiation. The pastor has been charged with felony child abuse. This case highlights the importance of contemporary Christians making a distinction between acknowledging the reality of the demonic, and acting superstitiously to exorcise "demons" for diagnosable medical conditions. Autism is not God's will for a child, and so is an example of the fallen nature of the creation, but autistic people are not possessed by demons.

New York Times online version, <nytimes.com>, August 29, 2003.

Transportation For The Mobility Impaired

Christians around the world help build PETs (Personal Energy Transportation). PETs are small three-wheeled carts that are propelled by hand. People with impaired mobility from polio, injury, land mine explosions, or other reasons can use them to go to work, take care of children and just to get out and around. Often, retired church members will build PETs as a ministry. PETs have been shipped to at least 27 countries, helping people earn a living and regain their dignity. One recipient remarked upon his first ride,

"For the first time in eight years, I am able to look people in the face instead of swallowing dust in the street." He had lost both legs to illness and had gotten around on a board with wheels.

Website: <www.giftofmobility.org>.

Paralyzed Woman Regains Mobility

Pam Morgan was severely injured on June 4, 2000. She and her husband, Phil, both professional gospel singers, were in their van with their two children when Phil nodded off, momentarily. The crash broke Phil's collarbone, and left the children with scratches. Pam, however, was thrown from the vehicle. Her spine was badly damaged. Dr. Frank Coufal, a neurosurgeon who treated Pam, told her husband that she would never walk again. With faith and prayer, Pam defied the expectations of the physicians. In Dr. Coufal's words, "There should have been no chance for her to have any functional recovery. To have clinical evidence of a complete spinal cord injury beyond three days of the time of injury and then to walk again is essentially unprecedented." Pam, and all of her family, prayed. E-mails offering prayer came from around the world. One day the couple's professional manager noticed that Pam could move her toe. Day-by-day more feeling returned, until the day came for her to try to walk with the aid of the parallel bars. Finally, several months after the accident, Pam walked unassisted into Dr. Coufal's office. Her next goal is to dance!

James A. Fussell, "Do Miracles Really Happen? Paralyzed United Methodist Woman Walks, Confounds Doctor," *United Methodist Reporter*, date unknown.

A Spiritual Healing

Margaret Kim Peterson, a theologian, tells of her husband's experience finding spiritual healing while he died of AIDS. Her husband, Hyung Goo, had returned to the Christian faith after a time of searching away from the church. Their pastor arranged a healing service at the church. Between thirty and forty people attended, including the members of their Bible study group. In the days leading up to the service, they both pondered some serious questions. They wondered whether they believed God could, or

138

would, heal Hyung Goo. They felt some anger at God for his illness in the first place. They even feared that the service would lead to despair if he prayed for healing, but didn't receive it. Although Hyung Goo's AIDS was not cured, both he and his wife experienced healing. They celebrated the friends who came to the service, and rejoiced over their marriage. Peterson could see the love in his face each time he looked at her. He found peace and freedom from a depression that had hung over him for much of his life. As Peterson puts it, "In a way as undeniable as it was mysterious, Hyung Goo was more whole when he died than he had been at any other time in his life."

"Healed, not Cured," *Christian Century*, 120.17, August 23, 2003, pp. 26-30.

Pastor's Seeing Eye Dog Commissioned For Ministry

Gene, a Seeing Eye dog for Reverend Eric Pridmore, was commissioned for ministry in the Mississippi Annual Conference of the United Methodist Church on June 3, 2004. Gene, a Golden Retriever, wore a stole during the ceremony when Pridmore was ordained an elder. Bishop Kenneth L. Carder, who ordained Pridmore, and commissioned Gene, said that Gene was a gift of God, enabling Pridmore to perform his ministry effectively. Of the ordination and commissioning service, Pridmore said, "It was nice to have the church, which disregards disabled folks at times, willing to acknowledge me as a servant of God just as I am."

Woody Woodrick, "Bishop Commissions Pastor's Faithful Guide," *United Methodist Reporter*, July 16, 2004, pp. 2-3.

Reading Our Bodies

Mary C. Earle, an Episcopal priest and retreat director, advocates that people with illnesses, injuries, and broken bodies read their bodies like a text. Earle suggests that bodily ailments can be interpreted using a method similar to the Rule of Saint Benedict, a time-honored way of studying the scriptures. By means of silence, meditation, and contemplation, we can read our bodies for insight and spiritual growth. This reading is a kind of practice of sabbath, of spending time remembering our relationship to God and resting in God. Earle affirms that an honest reading of illness can enable us to counteract facile and punitive interpretations of an illness or injury. In Earle's words, "The body is neither the betrayer nor the machine but a sacramental sign of the creating, redeeming, sanctifying work of God. We become aware that our bodies are not in our complete control; at the same time we have a call to be good stewards of these bodies, to care for them as good gifts from a good God — even when the bodies are afflicted and pain-stricken."

Mary C. Earle, *Broken Body, Healing Spirit: Lectio Divina and Living with Illness* (Harrisburg: Morehouse Publishing, 2003), p. 38.

Vandals Damage Health Clinic

A church-related health clinic in Phoenix was damaged in a senseless attack recently. The clinic, Centro de Salud, provided basic health services to low-income families. The vandals ruined equipment and medicine, sprayed fire extinguishers, and ransacked every room in the clinic. The damage was estimated at $25,000. At the time of the report no arrests had been made and no motive is known. The attack seems demonic because the vandals set back God's will for health and wholeness. It was likely a spasm of purposeless destruction that intended only harm.

Website: <www.wesleycenterphx.org>.

Pastor Healed At Conference

The Reverend David Zona suffered for three years with myasthenia gravis, a malady involving his immune and neuromuscular system. One primary symptom was chronic fatigue and shortness of breath. He was hospitalized several times for the disorder. Zona and his wife attended an "Aldersgate Conference on the Holy Spirit" in Springfield, Illinois, in 2003. Although he was moved by the worship services, he almost skipped the closing service [ironic note: John Wesley went "reluctantly" to his own Aldersgate experience]. At the end of the service, Zona felt called to go to the front for prayer. At the altar a woman reached out to lay hands on him. Zona reports that he felt a spiritual power even before her fingers touched him (see Mark 5:28-29). A few weeks later, Zona woke from sleep hearing the words, "You are healed." At a subsequent visit to his physician, Zona discovered that his symptoms were gone. Following this experience, Zona has ice skated with one son and coached soccer with the other.

Jan Woodard, "UM Pastor Experiences Healing After Conference," *United Methodist Reporter*, July 23, 2004, p. 3.

A Dramatic Change In Demeanor

Reverend Lois Cooper was engaged in volunteer ministry at Mountain View Prison for Women in Gatesville, Texas a few years ago. Following a meeting, one of the women inmates began shouting, screaming, and crying. Her body was writhing. Reverend Cooper and another pastor, Ella, went over to the woman. The other inmates explained that the woman was grieving the death of her mother. Reverend Cooper sensed something more than grief in the room. Ella directed some of the other women to help the convulsing woman to the floor, and exhorted everyone else except her, Lois, and one other minister to leave the room. Ella prayed for the woman and used what could be considered exorcistic language: "Let go, let God in." After a few minutes, the convulsing woman screamed loudly and all of her bodily movement stopped. The woman relaxed. Lois felt a sense of terror, and a kind of "electricity" in the room. Lois' scalp tingled. Lois and Ella spoke soothing words to the woman and Ella proclaimed, "It's gone." This experience is open to interpretation, but so is all of the evil of creation.

Reverend Cooper is pastor-in-residence at Cornerstone United Methodist Church in Garland, Texas. She related this incident to the author in a personal conversation.

Blind Man Rebuilds His Life

Rick Grunbaum of Dallas lost most of his eyesight when the cover of a swimming pool filter exploded in his face in January of 1995. Following the accident he was depressed. He lost his zest for living. He began to rebuild his life when a friend gave him a short-term membership to a health club. The training and exercise at the club gave him a new passion. He describes the effect of running and working out as spiritually uplifting. With hard work he qualified for the Boston marathon in 2003. He says of his struggle with blindness, "I had lost my previous life and started a new one. What it [exercise] does for you emotionally and spiritually is incredible."

Debbie Fetterman, "Running His Life," *The Dallas Morning News*, Sunday, April 20, 2003, p. 5C.

Turning Point In Battle For Life

Gregory Marshall was born with a condition in which his body does not produce enough of a particular white blood cell. At about the age of six, Gregory was near death. He was in the ICU, as close to the nurse's station as possible because of the severity of his condition. He had contracted viral pneumonia and was not expected to live. His lungs had nearly filled with fluid. Testing had indicated that he qualified for a new experimental treatment used only when all other hope had been exhausted. A member of Gregory's church was a nurse at the hospital on the night he was so close to death. She called her husband, John. Gregory's mother, Lisa, refers to John as a "spirit-filled" man. Arriving at the hospital, he offered to pray and encouraged the ICU nurses to pray, also. He placed Lisa's hand and his own hand on Gregory's head, telling Lisa to "pray as only a mother can pray." As John and Lisa were praying, Lisa felt a dramatic change in the room. She considers the change to have been the Lord's presence. The nurses commented on the change in the room as well. An hour later, Gregory began to improve. By the end of the night, the tests indicated that he no longer needed the new experimental treatment. The evening marked a turning point in Gregory's recovery. Five years later, Gregory still has health problems, but he is an artistic young man who is active at Cornerstone United Methodist Church and participates in scouts.

Lisa Marshall related this incident to the author in a personal conversation.

Suggestions For Further Reading

Achtemeier, Paul J. *Mark*. Philadelphia: Fortress Press, 1986.

Black, Kathy. *A Healing Homiletic: Preaching and Disability*. Nashville: Abingdon Press, 1996.

Brown, Raymond E. *The Gospel According to John I-XII*, The Anchor Bible, ed. William Foxwell Albright and David Noel Freedman, no. 29. Garden City, New York: Doubleday, 1966.

Campbell, Charles L. *The Word Before the Powers: An Ethic of Preaching*. Louisville: Westminster John Knox Press, 2002.

Davenport, Gene L. *Powers and Principalities*. Cleveland: The Pilgrim Press, 2003.

Donahue, John R. and Daniel J. Harrington. *The Gospel of Mark*, Sacra Pagina, ed. Daniel J. Harrington, no. 2. Collegeville: The Liturgical Press, 2002.

Eiseland, Nancy L. *The Disabled God: Toward a Liberatory Theology of Disability*. Nashville: Abingdon Press, 1994.

Hare, Douglas R. *Mark*, Westminster Bible Companion, ed. Patrick Miller and David L. Bartlett. Lousiville: Westminster John Knox Press, 1996.

Howard, Virgil and David B. Peabody. "Mark," in *The International Bible Commentary*, ed. William R. Farmer, 1331-1367. Collegeville, Minnesota; The Liturgical Press, 1998.

Kysar, Robert. *Preaching John*. Minneapolis: Fortress Press, 2002.

Levine, Amy-Jill, ed. *A Feminist Companion to Mark*. Sheffield: Sheffield Academic Press, 2001.

Maloney Francis J. *The Gospel of John*, Sacra Pagina, ed. Daniel J. Harrington, no. 4. Collegeville, Minnesota: The Liturgical Press, 1998.

Marcus, Joel. *Mark 1-8*, The Anchor Bible, ed. William Foxwell Albright and David Noel Freedman, no. 27. New York: Doubleday, 1999.

Myers, Ched. *Binding the Strong Man: A Political Reading of Mark's Story of Jesus*. Maryknoll: Orbis Books, 1988.

Reid, Robert Stephen. *Preaching Mark*. St. Louis: Chalice Press, 1999.